Oster Digital Countertop Convection Oven Cookbook

250 Easy and Quick Delicious Air Fryer Oven Recipes for Your New Oster Digital Convection Oven| Bake, Fry, Roast Crisp Recipes for Your Whole Family

By Onivis Brilank

Legal & Disclaimer

The information contained in this book and its contents is not designed to replace or take the place of any form of medical or professional advice; and is not meant to replace the need for independent medical, financial, legal or other professional advice or services, as may be required. The content and information in this book has been provided for educational and entertainment purposes only.

The content and information contained in this book has been compiled from sources deemed reliable, and it is accurate to the best of the Author's knowledge, information and belief. However, the Author cannot guarantee its accuracy and validity and cannot be held liable for any errors and/or omissions. Further, changes are periodically made to this book as and when needed. Where appropriate and/or necessary, you must consult a professional (including but not limited to your doctor, attorney, financial advisor or such other professional advisor) before using any of the suggested remedies, techniques, or information in this book.

Table of Content

Introduction

I have always hated cooking for as long as I can remember. Left to me, my husband and I should just have some coffee and pretzels for breakfast and canned beans and wine for dinner, but I can already hear the complaints about healthy food. Don't worry, I am a pro-healthy diet person now, and I enjoy making sure that my family eats only healthy meals.

Cooking can be a very complicated project. You first have to go to the mall to get stuff and know how to use every component of that recipe the right way. Then you have to use the ideal techniques and appropriate temperature while standing there and with your stomach growling.

For one, I have made many of my bad decisions while cooking, waiting for the food to be ready so that I could finally eat. What could be worse than cooking? Well, it turns out baking is even worse.

With baking, you get all covered in white powder. Then you have to nurture the yeast to live (have I ever mentioned how unpredictable yeast can be), then put the batter or dough in the oven and bake at a particular temperature for a specific amount of time. I can't remember making a good enough bake before I got the Oster, but that's a story for another day.

How I Discovered Oster Digital Countertop Oven?

So my husband and I have been getting take-outs and a heap of junk food to fuel our mutual dislike of the kitchen, but last year I resolved to overcome my aversion to the kitchen and start cooking again.

The first thing on my mind was to get was a cooker or an oven that could make the whole cooking process more straightforward, less stressful, and more enjoyable. After reading lots of reviews online and asking friends for their opinion, I finally decided to go on amazon and get the Oster Digital Convection Oven. It might just have been my best purchase decision of the year.

I was skeptical at first (I am actively suspicious of anything remotely involving cooking), but using the Oster oven has me convinced of its quality and reliability. I didn't believe the day would come when I will willingly start cooking, but the Oster Digital Countertop Convection Oven has proved me wrong.

The Oster Digital countertop oven has:

- Double racks; This increases cooking flexibility, which you can use to make a larger quantity simultaneously.

- An easily removable tray that makes it easier to remove those stubborn crumbs that manage to find their way into everything.

- A Patent made Turbo Convection technology that cooks way faster than my previous oven at an adjustable temperature.

The Oster was specially built for people like me who desperately want to get started cooking but are looking for a very superior and exciting kitchen experience.

The Oster oven has many different preset settings for cooking (Pizza, bake, broil, toast, defrost settings), all designed to make life easier for you. All you need to do is to set the mode you want, and the Oster will provide the necessary temperature conditions to get your food ready in record time.

Unlike other ovens, the Oster does not heat up your kitchen; its heat is restricted to the area directly near it. One of my neighbors had an oven explosion (luckily, no one was around then), so I am well aware of the benefits of using a safe oven.

When my husband and I decided to start cooking and eating right, I downloaded some recipes I could try. I even invented some badass recipes to explore, but I couldn't try all this on our old oven without it ruining my food and mood for the day.

I have prepared a variety of recipes that go with the Oster and are perfect for it. Some of which are paleo pizza, my famous Greek frittata, chicken quesadillas, spicy salmon sandwich, cheesy Lasagna toast, Lemon fish with chips, and my special extra moist carrot cake amongst others.

These recipes have been tried and adjusted to near perfection. I'm sure you'd find more than a few favorites.

You will agree that trying out recipes with a slow or malfunctioning cooker is just setting yourself up for disappointment and frustration. How are you supposed to be happy when your recipes turn out slightly burnt than usual or come out only half done?

Why Do You Need the Oster Digital Countertop Convectional Oven?

This book is a compilation of my best recipes that have repeatedly warmed the heart of my family and friends. From a simple serving of cheesy baked potatoes to a juicy full chicken and veggies platter, all recipes in this book can be made with your Oster digital countertop oven. What better way to wear your chef hat than with a secure device that makes each dish effortless? Here are some things Oster Digital Countertop Oven has to offer:

Oster Oven will Save You Energy

But I have been trying out the whole recipes I downloaded and dreamt of with the new Oster Countertop Convection Oven. To date, all of them have turned out good, well, except one where I made a mistake with the recipe and ended up with too much sugar in my cupcakes.

Overall, the cooking experience has been remarkable. Now I don't even get to worry about the recipe coming out great. I mix my batter and then put it in the oven; within minutes, the timer goes off, and my cake is ready to be sectioned.

Oster Oven will Save You Time

Another thing about the Oster is how fast it cooks stuff while still preserving the right amount of moisture. I had gotten used to my old way of using productive minutes to laze around the kitchen while the food was cooking, so imagine my surprise when I set pies into the Oster and set a timer, and it was ready by the correct time. With the Oster, you eliminate cooking time by more than half and enjoy a superior cooking experience that doesn't leave you anticipating a disaster about to happen.

Oster Oven is Big Enough for Your Dish

Talk about the holidays; the Oster Digital Countertop Convection Oven is just perfect for Christmas and Thanksgiving. Its large and roomy racks make it the ideal family oven to prepare roast chicken or fresh sizzling pies. Most people wrongfully think a countertop oven can't fit in a family-sized turkey or a pepperoni pizza. The Oster digital oven has a dimension of 21.65 "W x 19.29" D x 12.91" H, making it big enough to meet your needs.

The racks are even removable and adjustable if you want to make room for a slightly bigger than thy usual cooking size.

Have I ever mentioned that the oven has a 90-minute timer with an auto shut-off component that lets you know when your food is ready? This feature gives me the peace of mind that is hard to find with other cookers that have the possibility of burning your house down.

Oster Oven is Small Enough to Move Around

Another safety feature I love is its portability, which significantly conserves space.

You don't have to have a large state of the art kitchen to make amazing recipes. The Oster countertop oven can fit easily without requiring too much space.

Additionally, It's not like your conventional oven that is easily accessed by kids. Hosting my children's playdates is always a blast until I have to run around stopping the kids from pressing anything that remotely resembles a button. With the Oster Digital Countertop Oven, you have the option of changing its position to a counter that your kids can't reach. Out of sight, out of mind, and you can go about your day knowing your able cooking companion doesn't pose a threat to your children.

Oster Oven is Safe Enough for Your Home

The other day, hubby and I were trying out Roast Turkey baked sweet potatoes, and after putting it in the oven, we totally forgot about it while discussing work and other issues. When I finally remembered that we had something cooking, it was already too late, and I rushed off to the Oven with a dread of having burnt food for dinner. Imagine my surprise when the oven was already off, and my pretzels were just there sitting pretty and well-cooked.

That's the power you unlock with the Oster Digital Countertop Convection Oven, the privilege of not worrying about your food being burnt or taking twice the time to get into your belly. The Oster has been a lifesaver since day one, and you would do well to get it because it removes all the stress from cooking and makes it quite enjoyable.

Chapter 1 Sauces, Dips, and Dressings

Maple-Ketchup Ginger Sauce

Prep time: 5 minutes | Cook time: 5 minutes | Makes ²/₃ cup

3 tablespoons ketchup
2 tablespoons water
2 tablespoons maple syrup
1 tablespoon rice vinegar
2 teaspoons peeled

minced fresh ginger root
2 teaspoons soy sauce (or tamari, which is a gluten-free option)
1 teaspoon cornstarch

1. In a small saucepan over medium heat, combine all the ingredients and stir continuously for 5 minutes, or until slightly thickened. Enjoy warm or cold.

Vinegary Tahini Hemp Dressing

Prep time: 5 minutes | Cook time: 0 minutes | Makes 12 tablespoons

½ cup white wine vinegar
¼ cup tahini
¼ cup water
1 tablespoon hemp seeds
½ tablespoon freshly squeezed lemon juice
1 teaspoon garlic powder
1 teaspoon dried

oregano
1 teaspoon dried basil
1 teaspoon red pepper flakes
½ teaspoon onion powder
½ teaspoon pink Himalayan salt
½ teaspoon freshly ground black pepper

1. In a bowl, combine all the ingredients and whisk until mixed well.

Tahini-Lemon Chickpea Spread

Prep time: 5 minutes | Cook time: 0 minutes | Serves 2

1 (19-ounce / 539-g) can chickpeas, drained and rinsed
¼ cup tahini
3 tablespoons cold water
2 tablespoons freshly squeezed lemon juice

1 garlic clove
½ teaspoon turmeric powder
⅛ teaspoon black pepper
Pinch pink Himalayan salt, to taste

1. Combine all the ingredients in a food processor and blend until smooth.

Apple Mushroom Gravy

Prep time: 5 minutes | Cook time: 10 minutes | Serves 4

2 cups vegetable broth
½ cup finely chopped mushrooms
2 tablespoons whole wheat flour
1 tablespoon unsweetened applesauce
1 teaspoon onion

powder
½ teaspoon dried thyme
¼ teaspoon dried rosemary
⅛ teaspoon pink Himalayan salt
Freshly ground black pepper, to taste

1. In a nonstick saucepan over medium-high heat, combine all the ingredients and mix well. Bring to a boil, stirring frequently, reduce the heat to low, and simmer, stirring constantly, until it thickens.

Lemon-Garlic Tahini

Prep time: 5 minutes | Cook time: 0 minutes | Serves 4

¾ cup water
½ cup tahini
3 garlic cloves, minced

Juice of 3 lemons
½ teaspoon pink Himalayan salt

1. In a bowl, whisk together all the ingredients until mixed well.

Red Chile-Garlic Buffalo Sauce

Prep time: 5 minutes | Cook time: 20 minutes | Makes 2 cups

¼ cup olive oil
4 garlic cloves, roughly chopped
1 (5-ounce / 142-g) small red onion, roughly chopped
6 red chiles, roughly chopped (about 2 ounces /

56 g in total)
1 cup water
½ cup apple cider vinegar
½ teaspoon salt
½ teaspoon freshly ground black pepper

1. In a large nonstick sauté pan, heat ¼ cup olive oil over medium-high heat. Once it's hot, add the garlic, onion, and chiles. Cook for 5 minutes, stirring occasionally, until onions are golden brown.
2. Add the water and bring to a boil. Cook for about 10 minutes or until the water has nearly evaporated.
3. Transfer the cooked onion and chile mixture to a food processor or blender and blend briefly to combine. Add the apple cider vinegar, salt, and pepper. Blend again for 30 seconds.
4. Using a mesh sieve, strain the sauce into a bowl. Use a spoon or spatula to scrape and press all the liquid from the pulp.

Chimichurri Sauce

Prep time: 15 minutes | Cook time: 0 minutes | Makes 2 cups

1 cup minced fresh parsley
½ cup minced fresh cilantro
¼ cup minced fresh mint leaves
¼ cup minced garlic (about 6 cloves)
2 tablespoons

minced fresh oregano leaves
1 teaspoon fine Himalayan salt
1 cup olive oil or avocado oil
½ cup red wine vinegar
Juice of 1 lemon

1. Thoroughly mix the parsley, cilantro, mint leaves, garlic, oregano leaves, and salt in a medium bowl. Add the olive oil, vinegar, and lemon juice and whisk to combine.
2. Store in an airtight container in the refrigerator and shake before using.
3. You can serve the chimichurri over vegetables, poultry, meats, and fish. It also can be used as a marinade, dipping sauce, or condiment.

Cilantro Jalapeño Tomato Salsa

Prep time: 5 minutes | Cook time: 0 minutes | Serves 2

3 large tomatoes, chopped
½ small red onion, diced
⅛ cup chopped fresh cilantro
3 garlic cloves, chopped

2 tablespoons chopped pickled jalapeño pepper
1 tablespoon lime juice
¼ teaspoon pink Himalayan salt (optional)

1. In a medium bowl, combine all the ingredients and mix with a wooden spoon.

Coconut Lemon Dressing

Prep time: 5 minutes | Cook time: 0 minutes | Makes about 1 cup

8 ounces (227 g) plain coconut yogurt
2 tablespoons chopped fresh parsley
2 tablespoons

freshly squeezed lemon juice
1 tablespoon snipped fresh chives
½ teaspoon salt
Pinch freshly ground black pepper

1. Stir together the coconut yogurt, parsley, lemon juice, chives, salt, and pepper in a medium bowl until completely mixed.
2. Transfer to an airtight container and refrigerate until ready to use.
3. This dressing perfectly pairs with spring mix greens, grilled chicken or even your favorite salad.

Sesame Peanut Butter Sauce

Prep time: 10 minutes | Cook time: 0 minutes | Makes ²/₃ cup

½ cup natural peanut butter
4 teaspoons sesame oil
2 tablespoons rice vinegar
2 to 4 teaspoons freshly squeezed lime juice

2 to 2½ teaspoons hot sauce (optional)
1 teaspoon low-sodium soy sauce
1 teaspoon honey
1 teaspoon chopped peeled fresh ginger or pinch ground ginger

1. Place the peanut butter, sesame oil, and rice vinegar in a small bowl and stir until thoroughly mixed.
2. Whisk in the lime juice, hot sauce (if desired), soy sauce, honey, and ginger.
3. Store in an airtight container for up to 2 weeks and stir well before using.

Dijon Mixed Berry Vinaigrette

Prep time: 15 minutes | Cook time: 0 minutes | Makes about 1½ cups

1 cup mixed berries, thawed if frozen
½ cup balsamic vinegar
¹/₃ cup extra-virgin olive oil
2 tablespoons freshly squeezed lemon or lime juice
1 tablespoon lemon

or lime zest
1 tablespoon Dijon mustard
1 tablespoon raw honey or maple syrup
1 teaspoon salt
½ teaspoon freshly ground black pepper

1. Place all the ingredients in a blender and purée until thoroughly mixed and smooth.
2. You can serve it over a bed of greens, grilled meat, or fresh fruit salad.

Lime Garlic Tahini Dressing

Prep time: 5 minutes | Cook time: 0 minutes | Makes about ¾ cup

¹/₃ cup tahini
3 tablespoons filtered water
2 tablespoons freshly squeezed lime juice
1 tablespoon apple cider vinegar

1 teaspoon lime zest
1½ teaspoons honey
¼ teaspoon garlic powder
¼ teaspoon salt

1. Whisk together the tahini, water, vinegar, lime juice, lime zest, honey, salt, and garlic powder in a small bowl until well emulsified.
2. Serve immediately, or refrigerate in an airtight container for to 1 week.

Dill-Chive Ranch Dressing

Prep time: 5 minutes | Cook time: 0 minutes | Serves 8

1 cup plain Greek yogurt
¼ cup chopped fresh dill
2 tablespoons chopped fresh chives
Zest of 1 lemon

1 garlic clove, minced
½ teaspoon sea salt
⅛ teaspoon freshly cracked black pepper

1. Mix together the yogurt, dill, chives, lemon zest, garlic, sea salt, and pepper in a small bowl and whisk to combine.
2. Serve chilled.

Hot Remoulade Sauce

Prep time: 5 minutes | Cook time: 0 minutes | Serves 4

¾ cup mayonnaise
1 garlic clove, minced
2 tablespoons mustard
1 teaspoon horseradish

1 teaspoon Cajun seasoning
1 teaspoon dill pickle juice
½ teaspoon paprika
¼ teaspoon hot pepper sauce

1. Whisk together all the ingredients in a small bowl until completely mixed.
2. It can be used as a delicious dip for veggies, a sandwich or burger spread, or you can serve it with chicken fingers for a dipping sauce.

Dijon Honey Sauce

Prep time: 10 minutes | Cook time: 0 minutes | Makes about 1 cup

½ cup raw honey or maple syrup
½ cup Dijon mustard

1 teaspoon toasted sesame oil
1 garlic clove, minced

1. Whisk together all the ingredients in a small bowl until smooth.
2. Refrigerate to chill for at least 2 hours for best flavor.
3. This sauce can be served as a dip for fresh vegetables or a spread for wraps and sandwiches. It's perfect for salads, grilled or roasted meats.

Chapter 2 Breakfasts

Halloumi Pepper and Spinach Omelet

Prep time: 10 minutes | Cook time: 13 minutes | Serves 2

2 teaspoons canola oil
4 eggs, whisked
3 tablespoons plain milk
1 teaspoon melted butter
1 red bell pepper, seeded and chopped
1 green bell pepper, seeded and chopped
1 white onion, finely chopped
½ cup baby spinach leaves, roughly chopped
½ cup Halloumi cheese, shaved
Kosher salt and freshly ground black pepper, to taste

1. Preheat the oven to 350ºF (177ºC).
2. Grease a baking pan with canola oil.
3. Put the remaining ingredients in the baking pan and stir well.
4. Transfer to the oven and bake for 13 minutes.
5. Serve warm.

Vanilla Cinnamon Toasts

Prep time: 5 minutes | Cook time: 4 minutes | Serves 4

1 tablespoon salted butter
2 teaspoons ground cinnamon
4 tablespoons sugar
½ teaspoon vanilla extract
10 bread slices

1. Preheat the oven to 380ºF (193ºC).
2. In a bowl, combine the butter, cinnamon, sugar, and vanilla extract. Spread onto the slices of bread.
3. Put the bread inside the oven and bake for 4 minutes or until golden brown.
4. Serve warm.

Vanilla Soufflé

Prep time: 10 minutes | Cook time: 22 minutes | Serves 4

$^1/_3$ cup butter, melted
¼ cup flour
1 cup milk
1 ounce (28 g) sugar
4 egg yolks
1 teaspoon vanilla extract
6 egg whites
1 teaspoon cream of tartar
Cooking spray

1. In a bowl, mix the butter and flour until a smooth consistency is achieved.
2. Pour the milk into a saucepan over medium-low heat. Add the sugar and allow to dissolve before raising the heat to boil the milk.
3. Pour in the flour and butter mixture and stir rigorously for 7 minutes to eliminate any lumps. Make sure the mixture thickens. Take off the heat and allow to cool for 15 minutes.
4. Preheat the oven to 320ºF (160ºC). Spritz 6 soufflé dishes with cooking spray.
5. Put the egg yolks and vanilla extract in a separate bowl and beat them together with a fork. Pour in the milk and combine well to incorporate everything.
6. In a smaller bowl mix the egg whites and cream of tartar with a fork. Fold into the egg yolks-milk mixture before adding in the flour mixture. Transfer equal amounts to the 6 soufflé dishes.
7. Put the dishes in the oven and bake for 15 minutes.
8. Serve warm.

Ricotta Spinach Omelet with Parsley

Prep time: 10 minutes | Cook time: 10 minutes | Serves 1

1 teaspoon olive oil
3 eggs
Salt and ground black pepper, to taste
1 tablespoon ricotta
cheese
¼ cup chopped spinach
1 tablespoon chopped parsley

1. Grease the baking pan with olive oil. Preheat the oven to 330ºF (166ºC).
2. In a bowl, beat the eggs with a fork and sprinkle salt and pepper.
3. Add the ricotta, spinach, and parsley and then transfer to the pan. Bake for 10 minutes or until the egg is set.
4. Serve warm.

Spinach Scrambled Eggs with Basil

Prep time: 10 minutes | Cook time: 10 minutes | Serves 2

2 tablespoons olive oil
4 eggs, whisked
5 ounces (142 g) fresh spinach, chopped
1 medium tomato, chopped
1 teaspoon fresh
lemon juice
½ teaspoon coarse salt
½ teaspoon ground black pepper
½ cup of fresh basil, roughly chopped

1. Grease a baking pan with the oil, tilting it to spread the oil around. Preheat the oven to 280ºF (138ºC).
2. Mix the remaining ingredients, apart from the basil leaves, whisking well until everything is completely combined.
3. Bake in the oven for 10 minutes.
4. Top with fresh basil leaves before serving.

Parmesan Ranch Onion Risotto

Prep time: 10 minutes | Cook time: 30 minutes | Serves 2

1 tablespoon olive oil
1 clove garlic, minced
1 tablespoon unsalted butter
1 onion, diced
¾ cup Arborio rice
2 cups chicken stock, boiling
½ cup Parmesan cheese, grated

1. Preheat the oven to 390ºF (199ºC).
2. Grease a round baking tin with olive oil and stir in the garlic, butter, and onion.
3. Transfer the tin to the oven and bake for 4 minutes. Add the rice and bake for 4 more minutes.
4. Turn the oven to 320ºF (160ºC) and pour in the chicken stock. Cover and bake for 22 minutes.
5. Scatter with cheese and serve.

Parmesan Egg and Sausage Muffins

Prep time: 5 minutes | Cook time: 20 minutes | Serves 4

6 ounces (170 g) Italian sausage, sliced
6 eggs
⅛ cup heavy cream
Salt and ground
black pepper, to taste
3 ounces (85 g) Parmesan cheese, grated

1. Preheat the oven to 350ºF (177ºC). Grease a muffin pan.
2. Put the sliced sausage in the muffin pan.
3. Beat the eggs with the cream in a bowl and season with salt and pepper.
4. Pour half of the mixture over the sausages in the pan.
5. Sprinkle with cheese and the remaining egg mixture.
6. Bake in the preheated oven for 20 minutes or until set.
7. Serve immediately.

Seed and Nut Muffins with Carrots

Prep time: 15 minutes | Cook time: 10 minutes | Makes 8 muffins

½ cup whole-wheat flour, plus 2 tablespoons
¼ cup oat bran
2 tablespoons flaxseed meal
¼ cup brown sugar
½ teaspoon baking soda
½ teaspoon baking powder
¼ teaspoon salt
½ teaspoon cinnamon
½ cup buttermilk
2 tablespoons
melted butter
1 egg
½ teaspoon pure vanilla extract
½ cup grated carrots
¼ cup chopped pecans
¼ cup chopped walnuts
1 tablespoon pumpkin seeds
1 tablespoon sunflower seeds
Cooking spray

Special Equipment:
16 foil muffin cups, paper liners removed

1. Preheat the oven to 330ºF (166ºC).
2. In a large bowl, stir together the flour, bran, flaxseed meal, sugar, baking soda, baking powder, salt, and cinnamon.
3. In a medium bowl, beat together the buttermilk, butter, egg, and vanilla. Pour into flour mixture and stir just until dry ingredients moisten. Do not beat.
4. Gently stir in carrots, nuts, and seeds.
5. Double up the foil cups so you have 8 total and spritz with cooking spray.
6. Put 4 foil cups in the baking pan and divide half the batter among them.
7. Bake for 10 minutes or until a toothpick inserted in center comes out clean.
8. Repeat step 7 to bake remaining 4 muffins.
9. Serve warm.

Oat Porridge with Chia Seeds

Prep time: 10 minutes | Cook time: 5 minutes | Serves 4

2 tablespoons peanut butter
4 tablespoons honey
1 tablespoon butter,
melted
4 cups milk
2 cups oats
1 cup chia seeds

1. Preheat the oven to 390ºF (199ºC).
2. Put the peanut butter, honey, butter, and milk in a bowl and stir to mix. Add the oats and chia seeds and stir.
3. Transfer the mixture to a bowl and bake in the oven for 5 minutes. Give another stir before serving.

Cheddar Onion Omelet

Prep time: 10 minutes | Cook time: 12 minutes | Serves 2

3 eggs
Salt and ground black pepper, to taste
½ teaspoons soy sauce
1 large onion, chopped
2 tablespoons grated Cheddar cheese
Cooking spray

1. Preheat the oven to 355ºF (179ºC).
2. In a bowl, whisk together the eggs, salt, pepper, and soy sauce.
3. Spritz the baking pan with cooking spray. Spread the chopped onion across the bottom of the pan, then transfer the pan to the oven.
4. Bake in the preheated oven for 6 minutes or until the onion is translucent.
5. Add the egg mixture on top of the onions to coat well. Add the cheese on top, then continue baking for another 6 minutes.
6. Allow to cool before serving.

Mozzarella Pepperoni Pizza

Prep time: 10 minutes | Cook time: 6 minutes | Serves 1

1 teaspoon olive oil
1 tablespoon pizza sauce
1 pita bread
6 pepperoni slices
¼ cup grated

Mozzarella cheese
¼ teaspoon garlic powder
¼ teaspoon dried oregano

1. Preheat the oven to 350ºF (177ºC). Grease the baking pan with olive oil.
2. Spread the pizza sauce on top of the pita bread. Put the pepperoni slices over the sauce, followed by the Mozzarella cheese.
3. Season with garlic powder and oregano.
4. Put the pita pizza inside the oven and place a trivet on top.
5. Bake in the preheated oven for 6 minutes and serve.

Havarti Asparagus Strata

Prep time: 10 minutes | Cook time: 14 to 19 minutes | Serves 4

6 asparagus spears, cut into 2-inch pieces
1 tablespoon water
2 slices whole-wheat bread, cut into ½-inch cubes
4 eggs
3 tablespoons whole milk
2 tablespoons

chopped flat-leaf parsley
½ cup grated Havarti or Swiss cheese
Pinch salt
Freshly ground black pepper, to taste
Cooking spray

1. Preheat the oven to 330ºF (166ºC).
2. Add the asparagus spears and 1 tablespoon of water in a baking pan. Bake for 3 to 5 minutes until crisp-tender. Remove the asparagus from the pan and drain on paper towels. Spritz the pan with cooking spray.
3. Place the bread and asparagus in the pan.
4. Whisk together the eggs and milk in a medium mixing bowl until creamy. Fold in the parsley, cheese, salt, and pepper and stir to combine. Pour this mixture into the baking pan.
5. Bake for 11 to 14 minutes or until the eggs are set and the top is lightly browned.
6. Let cool for 5 minutes before slicing and serving.

Cheddar Onion Hash Brown Casserole

Prep time: 15 minutes | Cook time: 30 minutes | Serves 4

3½ cups frozen hash browns, thawed
1 teaspoon salt
1 teaspoon freshly ground black pepper
3 tablespoons butter, melted

1 (10.5-ounce / 298-g) can cream of chicken soup
½ cup sour cream
1 cup minced onion
½ cup shredded sharp Cheddar cheese
Cooking spray

1. Put the hash browns in a large bowl and season with salt and black pepper. Add the melted butter, cream of chicken soup, and sour cream and stir until well incorporated. Mix in the minced onion and cheese and stir well.
2. Preheat the oven to 325ºF (163ºC). Spray a baking pan with cooking spray.
3. Spread the hash brown mixture evenly into the baking pan.
4. Place the pan in the oven and bake for 30 minutes until browned.
5. Cool for 5 minutes before serving.

Maple Blueberry Granola Cobbler

Prep time: 5 minutes | Cook time: 15 minutes | Serves 4

¾ teaspoon baking powder
⅓ cup whole-wheat pastry flour
Dash sea salt
⅓ cup unsweetened nondairy milk

2 tablespoons maple syrup
½ teaspoon vanilla
Cooking spray
½ cup blueberries
¼ cup granola
Nondairy yogurt, for topping (optional)

1. Preheat the fryer to 347ºF (175ºC). Spritz a baking pan with cooking spray.
2. Mix together the baking powder, flour, and salt in a medium bowl. Add the milk, maple syrup, and vanilla and whisk to combine.
3. Scrape the mixture into the prepared pan. Scatter the blueberries and granola on top.
4. Transfer the pan to the oven and bake for 15 minutes, or until the top begins to brown and a knife inserted in the center comes out clean.
5. Let the cobbler cool for 5 minutes and serve with a drizzle of nondairy yogurt.

Cheddar Ham and Tomato Sandwiches

Prep time: 5 minutes | Cook time: 8 minutes | Serves 2

1 teaspoon butter, softened
4 slices bread
4 slices smoked country ham

4 slices Cheddar cheese
4 thick slices tomato

1. Preheat the oven to 370ºF (188ºC).
2. Spoon ½ teaspoon of butter onto one side of 2 slices of bread and spread it all over.

3. Assemble the sandwiches: Top each of 2 slices of unbuttered bread with 2 slices of ham, 2 slices of cheese, and 2 slices of tomato. Place the remaining 2 slices of bread on top, butter-side up.
4. Arrange the sandwiches in the baking pan, buttered side down.
5. Bake for 8 minutes until the sandwiches are golden brown on both sides and the cheese has melted, flipping the sandwiches halfway through.
6. Allow to cool for 5 minutes before slicing to serve.

Gouda Egg-Bacon Bread Cups

Prep time: 10 minutes | Cook time: 8 to 12 minutes | Serves 4

4 (3-by-4-inch) crusty rolls
4 thin slices Gouda or Swiss cheese mini wedges
5 eggs
2 tablespoons heavy cream

3 strips precooked bacon, chopped
½ teaspoon dried thyme
Pinch salt
Freshly ground black pepper, to taste

1. Preheat the oven to 330ºF (166ºC).
2. On a clean work surface, cut the tops off the rolls. Using your fingers, remove the insides of the rolls to make bread cups, leaving a ½-inch shell. Place a slice of cheese onto each roll bottom.
3. Whisk together the eggs and heavy cream in a medium bowl until well combined. Fold in the bacon, thyme, salt, and pepper and stir well.
4. Scrape the egg mixture into the prepared bread cups.
5. Transfer the bread cups to the oven and bake for 8 to 12 minutes, or until the eggs are cooked to your preference.
6. Serve warm.

Blueberry Muffins

Prep time: 10 minutes | Cook time: 12 minutes | Makes 8 muffins

1⅓ cups flour	1 egg
½ cup sugar	½ cup milk
2 teaspoons baking powder	⅔ cup blueberries, fresh or frozen and thawed
¼ teaspoon salt	
⅓ cup canola oil	

1. Preheat the oven to 330ºF (166ºC).
2. In a medium bowl, stir together flour, sugar, baking powder, and salt.
3. In a separate bowl, combine oil, egg, and milk and mix well.
4. Add egg mixture to dry ingredients and stir just until moistened.
5. Gently stir in the blueberries.
6. Spoon batter evenly into parchment paper-lined muffin cups.
7. Put 4 muffin cups in the baking pan and bake for 12 minutes or until tops spring back when touched lightly.
8. Repeat previous step to bake remaining muffins.
9. Serve immediately.

Cheddar Veggie Bacon-Egg Casserole

Prep time: 10 minutes | Cook time: 14 minutes | Serves 4

6 slices bacon	green bell pepper
6 eggs	½ cup chopped onion
Salt and pepper, to taste	¾ cup shredded Cheddar cheese
Cooking spray	
½ cup chopped	

1. Place the bacon in a skillet over medium-high heat and cook each side for about 4 minutes until evenly crisp. Remove from the heat to a paper towel-lined plate to drain. Crumble it into small pieces and set aside.
2. Whisk the eggs with the salt and pepper in a medium bowl.
3. Preheat the oven to 400ºF (204ºC). Spritz a baking pan with cooking spray.
4. Place the whisked eggs, crumbled bacon, green bell pepper, and onion in the prepared pan. Bake in the preheated oven for 6 minutes.
5. Scatter the Cheddar cheese all over and bake for 2 minutes more.
6. Allow to sit for 5 minutes and serve on plates.

Yellow Cornmeal Pancake

Prep time: 10 minutes | Cook time: 10 to 12 minutes | Serves 4

1½ cups yellow cornmeal	1 cup whole or 2% milk
½ cup all-purpose flour	1 large egg, lightly beaten
2 tablespoons sugar	1 tablespoon butter, melted
1 teaspoon salt	Cooking spray
1 teaspoon baking powder	

1. Preheat the oven to 350ºF (177ºC). Line the baking pan with parchment paper.
2. Stir together the cornmeal, flour, sugar, salt, and baking powder in a large bowl. Mix in the milk, egg, and melted butter and whisk to combine.
3. Working in batches, drop tablespoonfuls of the batter onto the parchment paper for each pancake.
4. Spray the pancakes with cooking spray and bake for 3 minutes. Flip the pancakes, spray with cooking spray again, and bake for an additional 2 to 3 minutes.
5. Remove from the pan to a plate and repeat with the remaining batter.
6. Cool for 5 minutes and serve immediately.

Parmesan Bacon-Ham Cups

Prep time: 5 minutes | Cook time: 20 minutes | Serves 2

3 slices bacon, cooked, sliced in half
2 slices ham
1 slice tomato
2 eggs

2 teaspoons grated Parmesan cheese
Salt and ground black pepper, to taste

1. Preheat the oven to 375ºF (191ºC). Line 2 greased muffin tins with 3 half-strips of bacon
2. Put one slice of ham and half slice of tomato in each muffin tin on top of the bacon
3. Crack one egg on top of the tomato in each muffin tin and sprinkle each with half a teaspoon of grated Parmesan cheese. Sprinkle with salt and ground black pepper, if desired.
4. Bake in the preheated oven for 20 minutes. Remove from the oven and let cool.
5. Serve warm.

Cheddar Baked Eggs

Prep time: 5 minutes | Cook time: 6 minutes | Serves 2

2 large eggs
2 tablespoons half-and-half
2 teaspoons shredded Cheddar

cheese
Salt and freshly ground black pepper, to taste
Cooking spray

1. Preheat the oven to 330ºF (166ºC).
2. Spritz 2 ramekins lightly with cooking spray. Crack an egg into each ramekin.
3. Top each egg with 1 tablespoon of half-and-half and 1 teaspoon of Cheddar cheese. Sprinkle with salt and black pepper. Stir the egg mixture with a fork until well combined.
4. Place the ramekins in the oven and bake for 6 minutes until set. Check for doneness and cook for 1 minute as needed.
5. Allow to cool for 5 minutes in the oven before removing and serving.

Chicken Sausage and Tater Tot Casserole

Prep time: 5 minutes | Cook time: 17 to 19 minutes | Serves 4

4 eggs
1 cup milk
Salt and pepper, to taste
12 ounces (340 g) ground chicken sausage

1 pound (454 g) frozen tater tots, thawed
¾ cup grated Cheddar cheese
Cooking spray

1. Whisk together the eggs and milk in a medium bowl. Season with salt and pepper to taste and stir until mixed. Set aside.
2. Place a skillet over medium-high heat and spritz with cooking spray. Place the ground sausage in the skillet and break it into smaller pieces with a spatula or spoon. Cook for 3 to 4 minutes until the sausage starts to brown, stirring occasionally. Remove from heat and set aside.
3. Preheat the oven to 400ºF (204ºC). Coat a baking pan with cooking spray.
4. Arrange the tater tots in the baking pan. Bake in the preheated oven for 6 minutes. Stir in the egg mixture and cooked sausage. Bake for another 6 minutes.
5. Scatter the cheese on top of the tater tots. Continue to bake for 2 to 3 minutes more until the cheese is bubbly and melted.
6. Let the mixture cool for 5 minutes and serve warm.

Buttermilk Biscuits

Prep time: 5 minutes | Cook time: 18 minutes | Makes 16 biscuits

2½ cups all-purpose flour
1 tablespoon baking powder
1 teaspoon kosher salt
1 teaspoon sugar
½ teaspoon baking soda
8 tablespoons (1 stick) unsalted butter, at room temperature
1 cup buttermilk, chilled

1. Stir together the flour, baking powder, salt, sugar, and baking powder in a large bowl.
2. Add the butter and stir to mix well. Pour in the buttermilk and stir with a rubber spatula just until incorporated.
3. Place the dough onto a lightly floured surface and roll the dough out to a disk, ½ inch thick. Cut out the biscuits with a 2-inch round cutter and re-roll any scraps until you have 16 biscuits.
4. Preheat the oven to 325ºF (163ºC).
5. Working in batches, arrange the biscuits in the baking pan in a single layer. Bake for about 18 minutes until the biscuits are golden brown.
6. Remove from the pan to a plate and repeat with the remaining biscuits.
7. Serve hot.

Cheddar Ham Hash Brown Cups

Prep time: 10 minutes | Cook time: 8 to 10 minutes | Serves 6

4 eggs, beaten
2¼ cups frozen hash browns, thawed
1 cup diced ham
½ cup shredded Cheddar cheese
½ teaspoon Cajun seasoning
Cooking spray

1. Preheat the oven to 350ºF (177ºC). Lightly spritz a 12-cup muffin tin with cooking spray.
2. Combine the beaten eggs, hash browns, diced ham, cheese, and Cajun seasoning in a medium bowl and stir until well blended.
3. Spoon a heaping 1½ tablespoons of egg mixture into each muffin cup.
4. Bake in the preheated oven for 8 to 10 minutes until the top is golden brown.
5. Allow to cool for 5 to 10 minutes on a wire rack and serve warm.

Vanilla Bourbon French Toast

Prep time: 15 minutes | Cook time: 6 minutes | Serves 4

2 large eggs
2 tablespoons water
⅔ cup whole or 2% milk
1 tablespoon butter, melted
2 tablespoons bourbon
1 teaspoon vanilla extract
8 (1-inch-thick) French bread slices
Cooking spray

1. Preheat the oven to 320ºF (160ºC). Line the baking pan with parchment paper and spray it with cooking spray.
2. Beat the eggs with the water in a shallow bowl until combined. Add the milk, melted butter, bourbon, and vanilla and stir to mix well.
3. Dredge 4 slices of bread in the batter, turning to coat both sides evenly. Transfer the bread slices onto the parchment paper.
4. Bake for 6 minutes until nicely browned. Flip the slices halfway through the cooking time.
5. Remove from the pan to a plate and repeat with the remaining 4 slices of bread.
6. Serve warm.

Egg in a Hole with Cheddar and Ham

Prep time: 5 minutes | Cook time: 5 minutes | Serves 1

1 slice bread
1 teaspoon butter, softened
1 egg
Salt and pepper, to taste
1 tablespoon shredded Cheddar cheese
2 teaspoons diced ham

1. Preheat the oven to 330ºF (166ºC). Place a baking dish in the oven.
2. On a flat work surface, cut a hole in the center of the bread slice with a 2½-inch-diameter biscuit cutter.
3. Spread the butter evenly on each side of the bread slice and transfer to the baking dish.
4. Crack the egg into the hole and season as desired with salt and pepper. Scatter the shredded cheese and diced ham on top.
5. Bake in the preheated oven for 5 minutes until the bread is lightly browned and the egg is cooked to your preference.
6. Remove from the oven and serve hot.

Brown Rice Porridge with Coconut and Dates

Prep time: 5 minutes | Cook time: 23 minutes | Serves 1 or 2

½ cup cooked brown rice
1 cup canned coconut milk
¼ cup unsweetened shredded coconut
¼ cup packed dark brown sugar
4 large Medjool
dates, pitted and roughly chopped
½ teaspoon kosher salt
¼ teaspoon ground cardamom
Heavy cream, for serving (optional)

1. Preheat the oven to 375ºF (191ºC).
2. Place all the ingredients except the heavy cream in a baking pan and stir until blended.
3. Transfer the pan to the oven and bake for about 23 minutes until the porridge is thick and creamy. Stir the porridge halfway through the cooking time.
4. Remove from the oven and ladle the porridge into bowls.
5. Serve hot with a drizzle of the cream, if desired.

Bacon-Cheese Muffin Sandwiches

Prep time: 5 minutes | Cook time: 8 minutes | Serves 4

4 English muffins, split
8 slices Canadian
bacon
4 slices cheese
Cooking spray

1. Preheat the oven to 370ºF (188ºC).
2. Make the sandwiches: Top each of 4 muffin halves with 2 slices of Canadian bacon, 1 slice of cheese, and finish with the remaining muffin half.
3. Put the sandwiches in the baking pan and spritz the tops with cooking spray.
4. Bake for 4 minutes. Flip the sandwiches and bake for another 4 minutes.
5. Divide the sandwiches among four plates and serve warm.

Chapter 3 Wraps and Sandwiches

Tilapia Tacos with Mayo

Prep time: 20 minutes | Cook time: 6 minutes | Serves 4

2 tablespoons milk
1/3 cup mayonnaise
1/4 teaspoon garlic powder
1 teaspoon chili powder
1½ cups panko bread crumbs
½ teaspoon salt
4 teaspoons canola oil
1 pound (454 g) skinless tilapia fillets, cut into 3-inch-long and 1-inch-wide strips
4 small flour tortillas
Lemon wedges, for topping
Cooking spray

1. Preheat the oven to 425ºF (218ºC). Spritz the baking pan with cooking spray.
2. Combine the milk, mayo, garlic powder, and chili powder in a bowl. Stir to mix well. Combine the panko with salt and canola oil in a separate bowl. Stir to mix well.
3. Dredge the tilapia strips in the milk mixture first, then dunk the strips in the panko mixture to coat well. Shake the excess off.
4. Arrange the tilapia strips in the pan. Bake for 6 minutes or until opaque on all sides and the panko is golden brown. Flip the strips halfway through. You may need to work in batches to avoid overcrowding.
5. Unfold the tortillas on a large plate, then divide the tilapia strips over the tortillas. Squeeze the lemon wedges on top before serving.

Beef Sloppy Joes

Prep time: 10 minutes | Cook time: 17 to 19 minutes | Makes 4 large sandwiches or 8 sliders

1 pound (454 g) very lean ground beef
1 teaspoon onion powder
1/3 cup ketchup
1/4 cup water
½ teaspoon celery seed
1 tablespoon lemon juice
1½ teaspoons brown sugar
1¼ teaspoons low-sodium Worcestershire sauce
½ teaspoon salt (optional)
½ teaspoon vinegar
1/8 teaspoon dry mustard
Hamburger or slider buns, for serving
Cooking spray

1. Preheat the oven to 390ºF (199ºC). Spray the baking pan with cooking spray.
2. Break raw ground beef into small chunks and pile into the pan. Bake for 5 minutes. Stir to break apart and bake for 3 minutes. Stir and bake for 2 to 4 minutes longer, or until meat is well done.
3. Remove the meat from the oven, drain, and use a knife and fork to crumble into small pieces.
4. Give your pan a quick rinse to remove any bits of meat.
5. Place all the remaining ingredients, except for the buns, in the pan and mix together. Add the meat and stir well.
6. Bake at 330ºF (166ºC) for 5 minutes. Stir and bake for 2 minutes.
7. Scoop onto buns. Serve hot.

Swiss Greens Sandwich

Prep time: 15 minutes | Cook time: 13 minutes | Serves 4

1½ cups chopped mixed greens
2 garlic cloves, thinly sliced
2 teaspoons olive oil
2 slices low-sodium low-fat Swiss cheese
4 slices low-sodium whole-wheat bread
Cooking spray

1. Preheat the oven to 425ºF (218ºC).
2. In a baking pan, mix the greens, garlic, and olive oil. Bake for 5 minutes, stirring once, until the vegetables are tender. Drain, if necessary.
3. Make 2 sandwiches, dividing half of the greens and 1 slice of Swiss cheese between 2 slices of bread. Lightly spray the outsides of the sandwiches with cooking spray.
4. Bake the sandwiches in the oven for 8 minutes, turning with tongs halfway through, until the bread is toasted and the cheese melts.
5. Cut each sandwich in half and serve.

Turkey Sliders with Chive Mayo

Prep time: 10 minutes | Cook time: 18 minutes | Serves 6

12 burger buns
Cooking spray
For the Turkey Sliders:
¾ pound (340 g) turkey, minced
1 tablespoon oyster sauce
¼ cup pickled jalapeno, chopped
2 tablespoons chopped scallions
1 tablespoon chopped fresh cilantro
1 to 2 cloves garlic, minced
Sea salt and ground black pepper, to taste
For the Chive Mayo:
1 tablespoon chives
1 cup mayonnaise
Zest of 1 lime
1 teaspoon salt

1. Preheat the oven to 380ºF (193ºC) and spritz the baking pan with cooking spray.
2. Combine the ingredients for the turkey sliders in a large bowl. Stir to mix well. Shape the mixture into 6 balls, then bash the balls into patties.
3. Arrange the patties in the pan and spritz with cooking spray. Bake for 18 minutes or until well browned. Flip the patties halfway through.
4. Meanwhile, combine the ingredients for the chive mayo in a small bowl. Stir to mix well.
5. Smear the patties with chive mayo, then assemble the patties between two buns to make the sliders. Serve immediately.

Colby Shrimp Sandwich with Mayo

Prep time: 10 minutes | Cook time: 7 minutes | Serves 4

1¼ cups shredded Colby, Cheddar, or Havarti cheese
1 (6-ounce / 170-g) can tiny shrimp, drained
3 tablespoons mayonnaise
2 tablespoons minced green onion
4 slices whole grain or whole-wheat bread
2 tablespoons softened butter

1. Preheat the oven to 425ºF (218ºC).
2. In a medium bowl, combine the cheese, shrimp, mayonnaise, and green onion, and mix well.
3. Spread this mixture on two of the slices of bread. Top with the other slices of bread to make two sandwiches. Spread the sandwiches lightly with butter.
4. Bake for 7 minutes, or until the bread is browned and crisp and the cheese is melted.
5. Cut in half and serve warm.

Turkey and Pepper Hamburger

Prep time: 10 minutes | Cook time: 20 minutes | Serves 4

1 cup leftover turkey, cut into bite-sized chunks
1 leek, sliced
1 Serrano pepper, deveined and chopped
2 bell peppers, deveined and chopped
2 tablespoons Tabasco sauce
½ cup sour cream

1 heaping tablespoon fresh cilantro, chopped
1 teaspoon hot paprika
¾ teaspoon kosher salt
½ teaspoon ground black pepper
4 hamburger buns
Cooking spray

1. Preheat the oven to 385ºF (196ºC). Spritz a baking pan with cooking spray.
2. Mix all the ingredients, except for the buns, in a large bowl. Toss to combine well.
3. Pour the mixture in the baking pan and place in the oven. Bake for 20 minutes or until the turkey is well browned and the leek is tender.
4. Assemble the hamburger buns with the turkey mixture and serve immediately.

Chicken and Lettuce Pita Sandwich

Prep time: 10 minutes | Cook time: 9 to 11 minutes | Serves 4

2 boneless, skinless chicken breasts, cut into 1-inch cubes
1 small red onion, sliced
1 red bell pepper, sliced
$1/_3$ cup Italian salad dressing, divided

½ teaspoon dried thyme
4 pita pockets, split
2 cups torn butter lettuce
1 cup chopped cherry tomatoes

1. Preheat the oven to 380ºF (193ºC).
2. Place the chicken, onion, and bell pepper in the baking pan. Drizzle with 1 tablespoon of the Italian salad dressing, add the thyme, and toss.
3. Bake for 9 to 11 minutes, or until the chicken is 165ºF (74ºC) on a food thermometer, stirring once during cooking time.
4. Transfer the chicken and vegetables to a bowl and toss with the remaining salad dressing.
5. Assemble sandwiches with the pita pockets, butter lettuce, and cherry tomatoes. Serve immediately.

Parmesan Eggplant Hoagies

Prep time: 15 minutes | Cook time: 14 minutes | Makes 3 hoagies

6 peeled eggplant slices (about ½ inch thick and 3 inches in diameter)
¼ cup jarred pizza sauce
6 tablespoons grated Parmesan cheese

3 Italian sub rolls, split open lengthwise, warmed
Cooking spray

1. Preheat the oven to 375ºF (191ºC) and spritz the baking pan with cooking spray.
2. Arrange the eggplant slices in the pan and spritz with cooking spray.
3. Bake for 12 minutes or until lightly wilted and tender. Flip the slices halfway through.
4. Divide and spread the pizza sauce and cheese on top of the eggplant slice and bake for 2 more minutes or until the cheese melts.
5. Assemble each sub roll with two slices of eggplant and serve immediately.

BBQ Bacon and Bell Pepper Sandwich

Prep time: 10 minutes | Cook time: 6 minutes | Serves 4

$1/_3$ cup spicy barbecue sauce
2 tablespoons honey
8 slices cooked bacon, cut into thirds
1 red bell pepper, sliced

1 yellow bell pepper, sliced
3 pita pockets, cut in half
1¼ cups torn butter lettuce leaves
2 tomatoes, sliced

1. Preheat the oven to 350ºF (177ºC).
2. In a small bowl, combine the barbecue sauce and the honey. Brush this mixture lightly onto the bacon slices and the red and yellow pepper slices.
3. Put the peppers into the baking pan and bake for 4 minutes. Add the bacon, and bake for 2 minutes or until the bacon is browned and the peppers are tender.
4. Fill the pita halves with the bacon, peppers, any remaining barbecue sauce, lettuce, and tomatoes, and serve immediately.

Mozzarella Chicken and Cabbage Sandwich

Prep time: 10 minutes | Cook time: 5 to 7 minutes | Serves 1

$1/_3$ cup chicken, cooked and shredded
2 Mozzarella slices
1 hamburger bun
¼ cup shredded cabbage
1 teaspoon mayonnaise
2 teaspoons butter, melted

1 teaspoon olive oil
½ teaspoon balsamic vinegar
¼ teaspoon smoked paprika
¼ teaspoon black pepper
¼ teaspoon garlic powder
Pinch of salt

1. Preheat the oven to 370ºF (188ºC).
2. Brush some butter onto the outside of the hamburger bun.
3. In a bowl, coat the chicken with the garlic powder, salt, pepper, and paprika.
4. In a separate bowl, stir together the mayonnaise, olive oil, cabbage, and balsamic vinegar to make coleslaw.
5. Slice the bun in two. Start building the sandwich, starting with the chicken, followed by the Mozzarella, the coleslaw, and finally the top bun.
6. Transfer the sandwich to the oven and bake for 5 to 7 minutes.
7. Serve immediately.

Chapter 4 Vegetables and Sides

Lemon-Garlic Broccoli

Prep time: 5 minutes | Cook time: 15 minutes | Serves 6

2 heads broccoli, cut into florets
2 teaspoons extra-virgin olive oil, plus more for coating
1 teaspoon salt
½ teaspoon black pepper
1 clove garlic, minced
½ teaspoon lemon juice

1. Cover the baking pan with aluminum foil and coat with a light brushing of oil.
2. Preheat the oven to 375ºF (191ºC).
3. In a bowl, combine all ingredients, save for the lemon juice, and transfer to the pan. Bake for 15 minutes.
4. Serve with the lemon juice.

Buffalo Cauliflower

Prep time: 5 minutes | Cook time: 5 minutes | Serves 1

½ packet dry ranch seasoning
2 tablespoons salted butter,
melted
1 cup cauliflower florets
¼ cup buffalo sauce

1. Preheat the oven to 400ºF (204ºC).
2. In a bowl, combine the dry ranch seasoning and butter. Toss with the cauliflower florets to coat and transfer them to the baking pan.
3. Bake for 5 minutes, stirring occasionally to ensure the florets bake evenly.
4. Remove the cauliflower from the oven, pour the buffalo sauce over it, and serve.

Curried Sweet Potato Fries

Prep time: 5 minutes | Cook time: 25 minutes | Serves 4

2 pounds (907 g) sweet potatoes, rinsed, sliced into matchsticks
1 teaspoon curry
powder
2 tablespoons olive oil
Salt, to taste

1. Preheat the oven to 390ºF (199ºC).
2. Drizzle the oil in the baking pan, place the fries inside and bake for 25 minutes.
3. Sprinkle with the curry powder and salt before serving.

Parmesan Broccoli with Shallot

Prep time: 5 minutes | Cook time: 4 minutes | Serves 4

1 pound (454 g) broccoli florets
1 medium shallot, minced
2 tablespoons olive oil
2 tablespoons
unsalted butter, melted
2 teaspoons minced garlic
¼ cup grated Parmesan cheese

1. Preheat the oven to 360ºF (182ºC).
2. Combine the broccoli florets with the shallot, olive oil, butter, garlic, and Parmesan cheese in a medium bowl and toss until the broccoli florets are thoroughly coated.
3. Arrange the broccoli florets in the baking pan in a single layer and bake for 4 minutes until crisp-tender.
4. Serve warm.

Baby Carrots with Honey Glaze

Prep time: 5 minutes | Cook time: 12 minutes | Serves 4

1 pound (454 g) baby carrots
2 tablespoons olive oil
1 tablespoon honey
1 teaspoon dried dill
Salt and black pepper, to taste

1. Preheat the oven to 350ºF (177ºC).
2. Place the carrots in a large bowl. Add the olive oil, honey, dill, salt, and pepper and toss to coat well.
3. Arrange the carrots in the baking pan and bake for 12 minutes until crisp-tender. Stir once during cooking.
4. Serve warm.

Russet Potatoes with Chives and Yogurt

Prep time: 5 minutes | Cook time: 35 minutes | Serves 4

4 (7-ounce / 198-g) russet potatoes, rinsed
Olive oil spray
½ teaspoon kosher salt, divided
½ cup 2% plain
Greek yogurt
¼ cup minced fresh chives
Freshly ground black pepper, to taste

1. Preheat the oven to 400ºF (204ºC).
2. Pat the potatoes dry and pierce them all over with a fork. Spritz the potatoes with olive oil spray. Sprinkle with ¼ teaspoon of the salt.
3. Put the potatoes in the baking pan and bake for 35 minutes until a knife can be inserted into the center of the potatoes easily.
4. Remove from the pan and split open the potatoes. Top with the yogurt, chives, the remaining ¼ teaspoon of salt, and finish with the black pepper. Serve immediately.

Garlic Eggplant Slices

Prep time: 5 minutes | Cook time: 15 minutes | Serves 1

1 large eggplant, sliced
2 tablespoons olive oil
¼ teaspoon salt
½ teaspoon garlic powder

1. Preheat the oven to 390ºF (199ºC).
2. Apply the olive oil to the slices with a brush, coating both sides. Season each side with sprinklings of salt and garlic powder.
3. Put the slices in the oven and bake for 15 minutes.
4. Serve immediately.

Mozzarella-Walnut Stuffed Portobellos

Prep time: 5 minutes | Cook time: 10 minutes | Serves 4

4 large portobello mushrooms
1 tablespoon canola oil
½ cup shredded Mozzarella cheese
$1/3$ cup minced walnuts
2 tablespoons chopped fresh parsley
Cooking spray

1. Preheat the oven to 350ºF (177ºC). Spritz the baking pan with cooking spray.
2. On a clean work surface, remove the mushroom stems. Scoop out the gills with a spoon and discard. Coat the mushrooms with canola oil. Top each mushroom evenly with the shredded Mozzarella cheese, followed by the minced walnuts.
3. Arrange the mushrooms in the pan and bake for 10 minutes until golden brown.
4. Transfer the mushrooms to a plate and sprinkle the parsley on top for garnish before serving.

Garlic Mustard Baked Veggies

Prep time: 10 minutes | Cook time: 7 minutes | Serves 4

1 large zucchini, sliced	herbs
1 cup cherry tomatoes, halved	1 teaspoon mustard
1 parsnip, sliced	1 teaspoon garlic purée
1 green pepper, sliced	6 tablespoons olive oil
1 carrot, sliced	Salt and ground black pepper, to taste
1 teaspoon mixed	

1. Preheat the oven to 425ºF (218ºC).
2. Combine all the ingredients in a bowl, making sure to coat the vegetables well.
3. Transfer to the oven and bake for 7 minutes, ensuring the vegetables are tender and browned.
4. Serve immediately.

Mushroom Pizza Squares with Shallot

Prep time: 10 minutes | Cook time: 10 minutes | Serves 10

1 pizza dough, cut into squares	chopped
1 cup chopped oyster mushrooms	2 tablespoons parsley
1 shallot, chopped	Salt and ground black pepper, to taste
¼ red bell pepper,	

1. Preheat the oven to 400ºF (204ºC).
2. In a bowl, combine the oyster mushrooms, shallot, bell pepper and parsley. Sprinkle some salt and pepper as desired.
3. Spread this mixture on top of the pizza squares.
4. Bake in the oven for 10 minutes.
5. Serve warm.

Chinese-Flavored Broccoli

Prep time: 5 minutes | Cook time: 10 minutes | Serves 2

12 ounces (340 g) broccoli florets	2 garlic cloves, finely chopped
2 tablespoons Asian hot chili oil	1 (2-inch) piece fresh ginger, peeled and finely chopped
1 teaspoon ground Sichuan peppercorns (or black pepper)	Kosher salt and freshly ground black pepper

1. Preheat the oven t0 375ºF (191ºC).
2. Toss the broccoli florets with the chili oil, Sichuan peppercorns, garlic, ginger, salt, and pepper in a mixing bowl until thoroughly coated.
3. Transfer the broccoli florets to the baking pan and bake for about 10 minutes, or until the broccoli florets are lightly browned and tender.
4. Remove the broccoli from the oven and serve on a plate.

Turnip and Zucchini with Garlic

Prep time: 5 minutes | Cook time: 15 to 20 minutes | Serves 4

3 turnips, sliced	crushed
1 large zucchini, sliced	1 tablespoon olive oil
1 large red onion, cut into rings	Salt and black pepper, to taste
2 cloves garlic,	

1. Preheat the oven to 330ºF (166ºC).
2. Put the turnips, zucchini, red onion, and garlic in a baking pan. Drizzle the olive oil over the top and sprinkle with the salt and pepper.
3. Place the baking pan in the preheated oven and bake for 15 to 20 minutes, or until the vegetables are tender.
4. Remove from the oven and serve on a plate.

Balsamic Carrots with Rosemary

Prep time: 5 minutes | Cook time: 18 minutes | Serves 3

3 medium-size carrots, cut into 2-inch × ½-inch sticks
1 tablespoon orange juice
2 teaspoons balsamic vinegar
1 teaspoon maple syrup
1 teaspoon avocado oil
½ teaspoon dried rosemary
¼ teaspoon sea salt
¼ teaspoon lemon zest

1. Preheat the oven to 392ºF (200ºC).
2. Put the carrots in the baking pan and sprinkle with the orange juice, balsamic vinegar, maple syrup, avocado oil, rosemary, sea salt, finished by the lemon zest. Toss well.
3. Bake for about 18 to 20 minutes until the carrots are nicely glazed and tender. Stir the carrots several times during the cooking process for even cooking.
4. Serve hot.

Cheddar Broccoli Gratin with Sage

Prep time: 5 minutes | Cook time: 12 to 14 minutes | Serves 2

¹/₃ cup fat-free milk
1 tablespoon all-purpose or gluten-free flour
½ tablespoon olive oil
½ teaspoon ground sage
¼ teaspoon kosher salt
⅛ teaspoon freshly ground black pepper
2 cups roughly chopped broccoli florets
6 tablespoons shredded Cheddar cheese
2 tablespoons panko bread crumbs
1 tablespoon grated Parmesan cheese
Olive oil spray

1. Preheat the oven to 330ºF (166ºC). Spritz a baking dish with olive oil spray.
2. Mix the milk, flour, olive oil, sage, salt, and pepper in a medium bowl and whisk to combine. Stir in the broccoli florets, Cheddar cheese, bread crumbs, and Parmesan cheese and toss to coat.
3. Pour the broccoli mixture into the prepared baking dish and place in the oven.
4. Bake for 12 to 14 minutes until the top is golden brown and the broccoli is tender.
5. Serve immediately.

Onion-Garlic Stuffed Mushrooms

Prep time: 5 minutes | Cook time: 12 minutes | Serves 2

18 medium-sized white mushrooms
1 small onion, peeled and chopped
4 garlic cloves, peeled and minced
2 tablespoons olive oil
2 teaspoons cumin powder
A pinch ground allspice
Fine sea salt and freshly ground black pepper, to taste

1. Preheat the oven to 345ºF (174ºC).
2. On a clean work surface, remove the mushroom stems. Using a spoon, scoop out the mushroom gills and discard.
3. Thoroughly combine the onion, garlic, olive oil, cumin powder, allspice, salt, and pepper in a mixing bowl. Stuff the mushrooms evenly with the mixture.
4. Place the stuffed mushrooms in the baking pan and bake for 12 minutes, or until the mushrooms are lightly browned on top.
5. Cool for 5 minutes before serving.

Sesame Carrots with Garlic

Prep time: 5 minutes | Cook time: 16 minutes | Serves 4 to 6

1 pound (454 g) baby carrots	Freshly ground black pepper, to taste
1 tablespoon sesame oil	6 cloves garlic, peeled
½ teaspoon dried dill	3 tablespoons sesame seeds
Pinch salt	

1. Preheat the oven to 380ºF (193ºC).
2. In a medium bowl, drizzle the baby carrots with the sesame oil. Sprinkle with the dill, salt, and pepper and toss to coat well.
3. Place the baby carrots in the baking pan and bake for 8 minutes.
4. Remove the pan and stir in the garlic. Return the pan to the oven and bake for another 8 minutes, or until the carrots are lightly browned.
5. Serve sprinkled with the sesame seeds.

Cauliflower with Garlic-Cilantro Sauce

Prep time: 15 minutes | Cook time: 20 minutes | Serves 4

Cauliflower:

5 cups cauliflower florets	cumin
3 tablespoons vegetable oil	½ teaspoon ground coriander
½ teaspoon ground	½ teaspoon kosher salt

Sauce:

½ cup Greek yogurt or sour cream	4 cloves garlic, peeled
¼ cup chopped fresh cilantro	½ teaspoon kosher salt
1 jalapeño, coarsely chopped	2 tablespoons water

1. Preheat the oven to 400ºF (204ºC).
2. In a large bowl, combine the cauliflower, oil, cumin, coriander, and salt. Toss to coat.
3. Put the cauliflower in the baking pan. Bake for 20 minutes, stirring halfway through the baking time.
4. Meanwhile, in a blender, combine the yogurt, cilantro, jalapeño, garlic, and salt. Blend, adding the water as needed to keep the blades moving and to thin the sauce.
5. At the end of baking time, transfer the cauliflower to a large serving bowl. Pour the sauce over and toss gently to coat. Serve immediately.

Broccoli and Potato with Tofu Scramble

Prep time: 15 minutes | Cook time: 36 minutes | Serves 3

2½ cups chopped red potato	powder
2 tablespoons olive oil, divided	½ teaspoon onion powder
1 block tofu, chopped finely	½ teaspoon garlic powder
2 tablespoons tamari	½ cup chopped onion
1 teaspoon turmeric	4 cups broccoli florets

1. Preheat the oven to 425ºF (218ºC).
2. Toss together the potatoes and 1 tablespoon of the olive oil.
3. Bake the potatoes in a baking dish for 18 minutes, stirring once during the cooking time to ensure they fry evenly.
4. Combine the tofu, the remaining 1 tablespoon of the olive oil, turmeric, onion powder, tamari, and garlic powder together, stirring in the onions, followed by the broccoli.
5. Top the potatoes with the tofu mixture and bake for an additional 18 minutes. Serve warm.

Breaded Cauliflower Patties

Prep time: 15 minutes | Cook time: 15 minutes | Serves 8

½ pound (227 g) cauliflower, steamed and diced, rinsed and drained
2 teaspoons coconut oil, melted
2 teaspoons minced garlic
¼ cup desiccated coconut
½ cup oats
3 tablespoons flour
1 tablespoon flaxseeds plus 3 tablespoons water, divided
1 teaspoon mustard powder
2 teaspoons thyme
2 teaspoons parsley
2 teaspoons chives
Salt and ground black pepper, to taste
1 cup bread crumbs

1. Preheat the oven to 425ºF (218ºC).
2. Combine the cauliflower with all the ingredients, except for the bread crumbs, incorporating everything well.
3. Using the hands, shape 8 equal-sized amounts of the mixture into burger patties. Coat the patties in bread crumbs before putting them in the baking pan in a single layer.
4. Bake for 15 minutes or until crispy.
5. Serve hot.

Corn Casserole with Swiss Cheese

Prep time: 5 minutes | Cook time: 15 minutes | Serves 4

2 cups frozen yellow corn
1 egg, beaten
3 tablespoons flour
½ cup grated Swiss or Havarti cheese
½ cup light cream
¼ cup milk
Pinch salt
Freshly ground black pepper, to taste
2 tablespoons butter, cut into cubes
Nonstick cooking spray

1. Preheat the oven to 320ºF (160ºC). Spritz a baking pan with nonstick cooking spray.
2. Stir together the remaining ingredients except the butter in a medium bowl until well incorporated.
3. Transfer the mixture to the prepared baking pan and scatter with the butter cubes.
4. Place the baking pan in the oven and bake for 15 minutes, or until the top is golden brown and a toothpick inserted in the center comes out clean.
5. Let the casserole cool for 5 minutes before slicing into wedges and serving.

Cream Cheese-Mayo Stuffed Bell Peppers

Prep time: 5 minutes | Cook time: 15 minutes | Serves 2

2 bell peppers, tops and seeds removed
Salt and pepper, to taste
$\frac{2}{3}$ cup cream cheese
2 tablespoons mayonnaise
1 tablespoon chopped fresh celery stalks
Cooking spray

1. Preheat the oven to 400ºF (204ºC). Spritz the baking pan with cooking spray.
2. Place the peppers in the pan and bake for 15 minutes, flipping the peppers halfway through, or until the peppers are crisp-tender.
3. Remove from the pan to a plate and season with salt and pepper.
4. Mix the cream cheese, mayo, and celery in a small bowl and stir to incorporate. Evenly stuff the baked peppers with the cream cheese mixture with a spoon. Serve immediately.

Provence Veggie Bake

Prep time: 20 minutes | Cook time: 30 minutes | Serves 4

1 sprig basil
1 sprig flat-leaf parsley
1 sprig mint
1 tablespoon coriander powder
1 teaspoon capers
½ lemon, juiced
Salt and ground black pepper, to taste
2 eggplants, sliced crosswise

2 red onions, chopped
4 cloves garlic, minced
2 red peppers, sliced crosswise
1 fennel bulb, sliced crosswise
3 large zucchinis, sliced crosswise
5 tablespoons olive oil
4 large tomatoes, chopped
2 teaspoons herbs de Provence

1. Blend the basil, parsley, coriander, mint, lemon juice and capers, with a little salt and pepper. Make sure all ingredients are well-incorporated.
2. Preheat the oven to 425°F (218°C).
3. Coat the eggplant, onions, garlic, peppers, fennel, and zucchini with olive oil.
4. Transfer the vegetables into a baking dish and top with the tomatoes and herb purée. Sprinkle with more salt and pepper, and the herbs de Provence.
5. Bake for 30 minutes.
6. Serve immediately.

Cornflakes-Crusted Tofu Sticks

Prep time: 5 minutes | Cook time: 17 minutes | Serves 4

2 tablespoons olive oil, divided
½ cup flour
½ cup crushed cornflakes

Salt and black pepper, to taste
14 ounces (397 g) firm tofu, cut into
½-inch-thick strips

1. Preheat the oven to 385°F (196°C). Grease the baking pan with 1 tablespoon of olive oil.
2. Combine the flour, cornflakes, salt, and pepper on a plate.
3. Dredge the tofu strips in the flour mixture until they are completely coated. Transfer the tofu strips to the greased pan.
4. Brush the remaining 1 tablespoon of olive oil over the top of tofu strips. Bake for 17 minutes until crispy, flipping the tofu strips halfway through.
5. Serve warm.

Potato, Carrot and Zucchini Bake

Prep time: 10 minutes | Cook time: 45 minutes | Serves 4

2 potatoes, peeled and cubed
4 carrots, cut into chunks
1 head broccoli, cut into florets
4 zucchinis, sliced thickly

Salt and ground black pepper, to taste
¼ cup olive oil
1 tablespoon dry onion powder

1. Preheat the oven to 400ºF (204ºC).
2. In a baking dish, add all the ingredients and combine well.
3. Bake for 45 minutes in the oven, ensuring the vegetables are soft and the sides have browned before serving.

Baked Veggie Salad with Chickpeas

Prep time: 5 minutes | Cook time: 20 minutes | Serves 2

1 potato, chopped
1 carrot, sliced diagonally
1 cup cherry tomatoes
½ small beetroot, sliced
¼ onion, sliced
½ teaspoon turmeric
½ teaspoon cumin
¼ teaspoon sea salt

2 tablespoons olive oil, divided
A handful of arugula
A handful of baby spinach
Juice of 1 lemon
3 tablespoons canned chickpeas, for serving
Parmesan shavings, for serving

1. Preheat the oven to 370ºF (188ºC).
2. Combine the potato, carrot, cherry tomatoes, beetroot, onion, turmeric, cumin, salt, and 1 tablespoon of olive oil in a large bowl and toss until well coated.
3. Arrange the veggies in the baking pan and bake for 20 minutes, stirring halfway through.
4. Let the veggies cool for 5 to 10 minutes in the pan.
5. Put the arugula, baby spinach, lemon juice, and remaining 1 tablespoon of olive oil in a salad bowl and stir to combine. Mix in the baked veggies and toss well.
6. Scatter the chickpeas and Parmesan shavings on top and serve immediately.

Cheesy Russet Potato Gratin

Prep time: 10 minutes | Cook time: 35 minutes | Serves 6

½ cup milk
7 medium russet potatoes, peeled
Salt, to taste
1 teaspoon black pepper

½ cup heavy whipping cream
½ cup grated semi-mature cheese
½ teaspoon nutmeg

1. Preheat the oven to 390ºF (199ºC).
2. Cut the potatoes into wafer-thin slices.
3. In a bowl, combine the milk and cream and sprinkle with salt, pepper, and nutmeg.
4. Use the milk mixture to coat the slices of potatoes. Put in a baking dish. Top the potatoes with the rest of the milk mixture.
5. Put the baking dish into the oven and bake for 25 minutes.
6. Pour the cheese over the potatoes.
7. Bake for an additional 10 minutes, ensuring the top is nicely browned before serving.

Chapter 5 Fish and Seafood

Tuna Casserole with Peppers

Prep time: 10 minutes | Cook time: 16 minutes | Serves 4

½ tablespoon sesame oil
¹/₃ cup yellow onions, chopped
½ bell pepper, seeded and chopped
2 cups canned tuna, chopped
Cooking spray
5 eggs, beaten
½ chili pepper, seeded and finely minced
1½ tablespoons sour cream
¹/₃ teaspoon dried basil
¹/₃ teaspoon dried oregano
Fine sea salt and ground black pepper, to taste

1. Heat the sesame oil in a nonstick skillet over medium heat until it shimmers.
2. Add the onions and bell pepper and sauté for 4 minutes, stirring occasionally, or until tender.
3. Add the canned tuna and keep stirring until the tuna is heated through.
4. Meanwhile, coat a baking dish lightly with cooking spray.
5. Transfer the tuna mixture to the baking dish, along with the beaten eggs, chili pepper, sour cream, basil, and oregano. Stir to combine well. Season with sea salt and black pepper.
6. Preheat the oven to 325ºF (160ºC).
7. Place the baking dish in the oven and bake for 12 minutes, or until the top is lightly browned and the eggs are completely set.
8. Remove from the oven and serve on a plate.

Almond-Lemon Crusted Fish

Prep time: 10 minutes | Cook time: 9 minutes | Serves 4

½ cup raw whole almonds
1 scallion, finely chopped
Grated zest and juice of 1 lemon
½ tablespoon extra-virgin olive oil
¾ teaspoon kosher salt, divided
Freshly ground black pepper, to taste
4 (6 ounces / 170 g each) skinless fish fillets
Cooking spray
1 teaspoon Dijon mustard

1. In a food processor, pulse the almonds to coarsely chop. Transfer to a small bowl and add the scallion, lemon zest, and olive oil. Season with ¼ teaspoon of the salt and pepper to taste and mix to combine.
2. Spray the top of the fish with oil and squeeze the lemon juice over the fish. Season with the remaining ½ teaspoon salt and pepper to taste. Spread the mustard on top of the fish. Dividing evenly, press the almond mixture onto the top of the fillets to adhere.
3. Preheat the oven to 400ºF (204ºC).
4. Working in batches, place the fillets in the baking pan in a single layer. Bake for 9 minutes, until the crumbs start to brown and the fish is cooked through.
5. Serve immediately.

Lemon-Caper Salmon Burgers

Prep time: 15 minutes | Cook time: 15 minutes | Serves 5

Lemon-Caper Rémoulade:

½ cup mayonnaise
2 tablespoons minced drained capers
2 tablespoons

chopped fresh parsley
2 teaspoons fresh lemon juice

Salmon Patties:

1 pound (454 g) wild salmon fillet, skinned and pin bones removed
6 tablespoons panko bread crumbs
¼ cup minced red onion plus ¼ cup slivered for serving
1 garlic clove, minced

1 large egg, lightly beaten
1 tablespoon Dijon mustard
1 teaspoon fresh lemon juice
1 tablespoon chopped fresh parsley
½ teaspoon kosher salt

For Serving:

5 whole wheat potato buns or gluten-free buns

10 butter lettuce leaves

1. For the lemon-caper rémoulade: In a small bowl, combine the mayonnaise, capers, parsley, and lemon juice and mix well.
2. For the salmon patties: Cut off a 4-ounce / 113-g piece of the salmon and transfer to a food processor. Pulse until it becomes pasty. With a sharp knife, chop the remaining salmon into small cubes.
3. In a medium bowl, combine the chopped and processed salmon with the panko, minced red onion, garlic, egg, mustard, lemon juice, parsley, and salt. Toss gently to combine. Form the mixture into 5 patties about ¾ inch thick. Refrigerate for at least 30 minutes.
4. Preheat the oven to 425ºF (218ºC).
5. Working in batches, place the patties in the baking pan. Bake for about 15 minutes, gently flipping halfway, until golden and cooked through.
6. To serve, transfer each patty to a bun. Top each with 2 lettuce leaves, 2 tablespoons of the rémoulade, and the slivered red onions.

Salmon and Carrot Spring Rolls

Prep time: 20 minutes | Cook time: 15 to 19 minutes | Serves 4

½ pound (227 g) salmon fillet
1 teaspoon toasted sesame oil
1 onion, sliced
1 carrot, shredded
1 yellow bell pepper, thinly sliced

⅓ cup chopped fresh flat-leaf parsley
¼ cup chopped fresh basil
8 rice paper wrappers

1. Preheat the oven to 370ºF (188ºC).
2. Arrange the salmon in the baking pan. Drizzle the sesame oil all over the salmon and scatter the onion on top. Bake for 8 to 10 minutes, or until the fish flakes when pressed lightly with a fork.
3. Meanwhile, fill a small shallow bowl with warm water. One by one, dip the rice paper wrappers into the water for a few seconds or just until moistened, then put them on a work surface.
4. Make the spring rolls: Place ⅛ of the salmon and onion mixture, carrot, bell pepper, parsley, and basil into the center of the rice wrapper and fold the sides over the filling. Roll up the wrapper carefully and tightly like you would a burrito. Repeat with the remaining wrappers and filling.
5. Transfer the rolls to the pan and bake at 380ºF (193ºC) for 7 to 9 minutes, or until the rolls are crispy and lightly browned.
6. Cut each roll in half and serve warm.

Italian-Style Salmon Patties

Prep time: 10 minutes | Cook time: 8 minutes | Serves 4

2 (5-ounce / 142 g) cans salmon, flaked
2 large eggs, beaten
⅓ cup minced onion
⅔ cup panko bread crumbs
1½ teaspoons Italian-Style seasoning
1 teaspoon garlic powder
Cooking spray

1. In a medium bowl, stir together the salmon, eggs, and onion.
2. In a small bowl, whisk the bread crumbs, Italian-Style seasoning, and garlic powder until blended. Add the bread crumb mixture to the salmon mixture and stir until blended. Shape the mixture into 8 patties.
3. Preheat the oven to 350ºF (177ºC). Line the baking pan with parchment paper.
4. Working in batches as needed, place the patties on the parchment and spritz with oil.
5. Bake for 4 minutes. Flip, spritz the patties with oil, and bake for 4 to 8 minutes more, until browned and firm. Serve.

Paprika Tilapia with Garlic Aioli

Prep time: 5 minutes | Cook time: 15 minutes | Serves 4

Tilapia:
4 tilapia fillets
1 tablespoon extra-virgin olive oil
1 teaspoon garlic powder
1 teaspoon paprika
1 teaspoon dried basil
A pinch of lemon-pepper seasoning
Garlic Aioli:
2 garlic cloves, minced
1 tablespoon mayonnaise
Juice of ½ lemon
1 teaspoon extra-virgin olive oil
Salt and pepper, to taste

1. Preheat the oven to 400ºF (204ºC).
2. On a clean work surface, brush both sides of each fillet with the olive oil. Sprinkle with the garlic powder, paprika, basil, and lemon-pepper seasoning.
3. Place the fillets in the baking pan and bake for 15 minutes, flipping the fillets halfway through, or until the fish flakes easily and is no longer translucent in the center.
4. Meanwhile, make the garlic aioli: Whisk together the garlic, mayo, lemon juice, olive oil, salt, and pepper in a small bowl until smooth.
5. Remove the fish from the pan and serve with the garlic aioli on the side.

Old Bay Salmon Patty Bites

Prep time: 15 minutes | Cook time: 15 minutes | Serves 4

4 (5-ounce / 142-g) cans pink salmon, skinless, boneless in water, drained
2 eggs, beaten
1 cup whole-wheat panko bread crumbs
4 tablespoons finely minced red bell pepper
2 tablespoons parsley flakes
2 teaspoons Old Bay seasoning
Cooking spray

1. Preheat the oven to 385ºF (196ºC).
2. Spray the baking pan lightly with cooking spray.
3. In a medium bowl, mix the salmon, eggs, panko bread crumbs, red bell pepper, parsley flakes, and Old Bay seasoning.
4. Using a small cookie scoop, form the mixture into 20 balls.
5. Place the salmon bites in the pan in a single layer and spray lightly with cooking spray. You may need to cook them in batches.
6. Bake for 15 minutes, stirring a couple of times for even cooking.
7. Serve immediately.

Trout Amandine with Lemon Butter Sauce

Prep time: 20 minutes | Cook time:8 minutes | Serves 4

Trout Amandine:

$^2/_3$ cup toasted almonds	pepper
$^1/_3$ cup grated Parmesan cheese	2 tablespoons butter, melted
1 teaspoon salt	4 (4-ounce / 113-g) trout fillets, or salmon fillets
½ teaspoon freshly ground black	Cooking spray

Lemon Butter Sauce:

8 tablespoons (1 stick) butter, melted	sauce
2 tablespoons freshly squeezed lemon juice	½ teaspoon salt
	½ teaspoon freshly ground black pepper
½ teaspoon Worcestershire	¼ teaspoon hot sauce

1. In a blender or food processor, pulse the almonds for 5 to 10 seconds until finely processed. Transfer to a shallow bowl and whisk in the Parmesan cheese, salt, and pepper. Place the melted butter in another shallow bowl.
2. One at a time, dip the fish in the melted butter, then the almond mixture, coating thoroughly.
3. Preheat the oven to 300ºF (149ºC). Line the baking pan with parchment paper.
4. Place the coated fish on the parchment and spritz with oil.
5. Bake for 4 minutes. Flip the fish, spritz it with oil, and bake for 4 minutes more until the fish flakes easily with a fork.
6. In a small bowl, whisk the butter, lemon juice, Worcestershire sauce, salt, pepper, and hot sauce until blended.
7. Serve with the fish.

Crab and Fish Cakes with Celery

Prep time: 20 minutes | Cook time: 10 to 12 minutes | Serves 4

8 ounces (227 g) imitation crab meat	saltine cracker crumbs
4 ounces (113 g) leftover cooked fish (such as cod, pollock, or haddock)	2 teaspoons dried parsley flakes
2 tablespoons minced celery	1 teaspoon prepared yellow mustard
2 tablespoons minced green onion	½ teaspoon garlic powder
2 tablespoons light mayonnaise	½ teaspoon dried dill weed, crushed
1 tablespoon plus 2 teaspoons Worcestershire sauce	½ teaspoon Old Bay seasoning
¾ cup crushed	½ cup panko bread crumbs
	Cooking spray

1. Preheat the oven to 390ºF (199ºC).
2. Pulse the crab meat and fish in a food processor until finely chopped.
3. Transfer the meat mixture to a large bowl, along with the celery, green onion, mayo, Worcestershire sauce, cracker crumbs, parsley flakes, mustard, garlic powder, dill weed, and Old Bay seasoning. Stir to mix well.
4. Scoop out the meat mixture and form into 8 equal-sized patties with your hands.
5. Place the panko bread crumbs on a plate. Roll the patties in the bread crumbs until they are evenly coated on both sides. Spritz the patties with cooking spray.
6. Put the patties in the baking pan and bake for 10 to 12 minutes, flipping them halfway through, or until they are golden brown and cooked through.
7. Divide the patties among four plates and serve.

Swordfish Steaks with Jalapeño

Prep time: 10 minutes | Cook time: 13 minutes | Serves 4

4 (4-ounce / 113-g) swordfish steaks
½ teaspoon toasted sesame oil
1 jalapeño pepper, finely minced
2 garlic cloves, grated
2 tablespoons freshly squeezed lemon juice
1 tablespoon grated fresh ginger
½ teaspoon Chinese five-spice powder
⅛ teaspoon freshly ground black pepper

1. On a clean work surface, place the swordfish steaks and brush both sides of the fish with the sesame oil.
2. Combine the jalapeño, garlic, lemon juice, ginger, five-spice powder, and black pepper in a small bowl and stir to mix well. Rub the mixture all over the fish until completely coated. Allow to sit for 10 minutes.
3. Preheat the oven to 410ºF (210ºC).
4. Arrange the swordfish steaks in the baking pan and bake for 13 minutes until cooked through, flipping the steaks halfway through.
5. Cool for 5 minutes before serving.

Almond-Coconut Flounder Fillets

Prep time: 8 minutes | Cook time: 12 minutes | Serves 2

2 flounder fillets, patted dry
1 egg
½ teaspoon Worcestershire sauce
¼ cup almond flour
¼ cup coconut flour
½ teaspoon coarse sea salt
½ teaspoon lemon pepper
¼ teaspoon chili powder
Cooking spray

1. Preheat the oven to 390ºF (199ºC). Spritz the baking pan with cooking spray.
2. In a shallow bowl, beat together the egg with Worcestershire sauce until well incorporated.
3. In another bowl, thoroughly combine the almond flour, coconut flour, sea salt, lemon pepper, and chili powder.
4. Dredge the fillets in the egg mixture, shaking off any excess, then roll in the flour mixture to coat well.
5. Place the fillets in the pan and bake for 7 minutes. Flip the fillets and spray with cooking spray. Continue cooking for 5 minutes, or until the fish is flaky.
6. Serve warm.

Baked Bacon-Wrapped Scallops

Prep time: 5 minutes | Cook time: 12 minutes | Serves 4

8 slices bacon, cut in half
16 sea scallops, patted dry
Cooking spray
Salt and freshly
ground black pepper, to taste
16 toothpicks, soaked in water for at least 30 minutes

1. Preheat the oven to 395ºF (202ºC).
2. On a clean work surface, wrap half of a slice of bacon around each scallop and secure with a toothpick.
3. Lay the bacon-wrapped scallops in the baking pan in a single layer. You may need to work in batches to avoid overcrowding.
4. Spritz the scallops with cooking spray and sprinkle the salt and pepper to season.
5. Bake for 12 minutes, flipping the scallops halfway through, or until the bacon is cooked through and the scallops are firm.
6. Remove the scallops from the oven to a plate and repeat with the remaining scallops. Serve warm.

Cajun Cod with Lemon Pepper

Prep time: 5 minutes | Cook time: 12 minutes | Makes 2 cod fillets

1 tablespoon Cajun seasoning
1 teaspoon salt
½ teaspoon lemon pepper
½ teaspoon freshly ground black pepper

2 (8-ounce / 227-g) cod fillets
Cooking spray
2 tablespoons unsalted butter, melted
1 lemon, cut into 4 wedges

1. Preheat the oven to 360°F (182°C). Spritz the baking pan with cooking spray.
2. Thoroughly combine the Cajun seasoning, salt, lemon pepper, and black pepper in a small bowl. Rub this mixture all over the cod fillets until completely coated.
3. Put the fillets in the pan and brush the melted butter over both sides of each fillet.
4. Bake in the preheated oven for 12 minutes, flipping the fillets halfway through, or until the fish flakes easily with a fork.
5. Remove the fillets from the oven and serve with fresh lemon wedges.

Breaded Calamari Rings with Lemon

Prep time: 5 minutes | Cook time: 12 minutes | Serves 4

2 large eggs
2 garlic cloves, minced
½ cup cornstarch
1 cup bread crumbs

1 pound (454 g) calamari rings
Cooking spray
1 lemon, sliced

1. In a small bowl, whisk the eggs with minced garlic. Place the cornstarch and bread crumbs into separate shallow dishes.
2. Dredge the calamari rings in the cornstarch, then dip in the egg mixture, shaking off any excess, finally roll them in the bread crumbs to coat well. Let the calamari rings sit for 10 minutes in the refrigerator.
3. Preheat the oven to 425°F (218°C). Spritz the baking pan with cooking spray.
4. Put the calamari rings in the pan and bake for 15 minutes until cooked through. Stir halfway through the cooking time.
5. Serve the calamari rings with the lemon slices sprinkled on top.

Breaded Fresh Scallops

Prep time: 5 minutes | Cook time: 10 minutes | Serves 4

1 egg
3 tablespoons flour
1 cup bread crumbs
1 pound (454 g) fresh scallops

2 tablespoons olive oil
Salt and black pepper, to taste

1. Preheat the oven to 385°F (196°C).
2. In a bowl, lightly beat the egg. Place the flour and bread crumbs into separate shallow dishes.
3. Dredge the scallops in the flour and shake off any excess. Dip the flour-coated scallops in the beaten egg and roll in the bread crumbs.
4. Brush the scallops generously with olive oil and season with salt and pepper, to taste.
5. Arrange the scallops in the baking pan and bake for 10 minutes, or until the scallops are firm and reach an internal temperature of just 145°F (63°C) on a meat thermometer. Stir halfway through the cooking time.
6. Let the scallops cool for 5 minutes and serve.

Garlic-Lemon Shrimp

Prep time: 10 minutes | Cook time: 14 minutes | Serves 4

2 teaspoons minced garlic
2 teaspoons lemon juice
2 teaspoons olive oil
½ to 1 teaspoon

crushed red pepper
12 ounces (340 g) medium shrimp, deveined, with tails on
Cooking spray

1. In a medium bowl, mix together the garlic, lemon juice, olive oil, and crushed red pepper to make a marinade.
2. Add the shrimp and toss to coat in the marinade. Cover with plastic wrap and place the bowl in the refrigerator for 30 minutes.
3. Preheat the oven to 425ºF (218ºC). Spray the baking pan lightly with cooking spray.
4. Place the shrimp in the pan. Bake for 6 minutes. Stir and bake until the shrimp are cooked through and nicely browned, an additional 8 minutes. Cool for 5 minutes before serving.

Cayenne Prawns with Cumin

Prep time: 10 minutes | Cook time: 10 minutes | Serves 2

8 prawns, cleaned
Salt and black pepper, to taste
½ teaspoon ground cayenne pepper
½ teaspoon garlic

powder
½ teaspoon ground cumin
½ teaspoon red chili flakes
Cooking spray

1. Preheat the oven to 375ºF (191ºC). Spritz the baking pan with cooking spray.
2. Toss the remaining ingredients in a large bowl until the prawns are well coated.

3. Spread the coated prawns evenly in the pan and spray them with cooking spray.
4. Bake for 10 minutes, flipping the prawns halfway through, or until the prawns are pink.
5. Remove the prawns from the pan to a plate.

Mustard-Lemon Sole Fillets

Prep time: 5 minutes | Cook time: 8 to 11 minutes | Serves 4

5 teaspoons low-sodium yellow mustard
1 tablespoon freshly squeezed lemon juice
4 (3.5-ounce / 99-g) sole fillets
2 teaspoons olive oil

½ teaspoon dried marjoram
½ teaspoon dried thyme
⅛ teaspoon freshly ground black pepper
1 slice low-sodium whole-wheat bread, crumbled

1. Preheat the oven to 320ºF (160ºC).
2. Whisk together the mustard and lemon juice in a small bowl until thoroughly mixed and smooth. Spread the mixture evenly over the sole fillets, then transfer to the baking pan.
3. In a separate bowl, combine the olive oil, marjoram, thyme, black pepper, and bread crumbs and stir to mix well. Gently but firmly press the mixture onto the top of fillets, coating them completely.
4. Bake in the preheated oven for 8 to 11 minutes, or until the internal temperature reaches 145ºF (63ºC) on a meat thermometer and the outer coating is crisp.
5. Remove from the oven and serve on a plate.

Tomato Chili Fish Curry

Prep time: 10 minutes | Cook time: 24 minutes | Serves 4

2 tablespoons sunflower oil	minced
1 pound (454 g) fish, chopped	1 cup coconut milk
	1 tablespoon coriander powder
1 ripe tomato, pureéd	1 teaspoon red curry paste
2 red chilies, chopped	½ teaspoon fenugreek seeds
1 shallot, minced	Salt and white pepper, to taste
1 garlic clove,	

1. Preheat the oven to 400ºF (204ºC). Coat the baking pan with the sunflower oil.
2. Place the fish in the pan and bake for 12 minutes. Flip the fish halfway through the cooking time.
3. When done, stir in the remaining ingredients and return to the oven.
4. Reduce the temperature to 350ºF (177ºC) and bake for another 12 minutes until heated through.
5. Cool for 5 to 8 minutes before serving.

Crab Ratatouille with Tomatoes and Eggplant

Prep time: 15 minutes | Cook time: 11 to 14 minutes | Serves 4

1½ cups peeled and cubed eggplant	basil
2 large tomatoes, chopped	½ teaspoon dried thyme
1 red bell pepper, chopped	Pinch salt
1 onion, chopped	Freshly ground black pepper, to taste
1 tablespoon olive oil	1½ cups cooked crab meat
½ teaspoon dried	

1. Preheat the oven to 400ºF (204ºC).
2. In a metal bowl, stir together the eggplant, tomatoes, bell pepper, onion, olive oil, basil and thyme. Season with salt and pepper.
3. Place the bowl in the preheated oven and bake for 9 minutes.
4. Remove the bowl from the oven. Add the crab meat and stir well and bake for another 2 to 5 minutes, or until the vegetables are softened and the ratatouille is bubbling.
5. Serve warm.

Smoked Paprika Salmon in White Wine

Prep time: 5 minutes | Cook time: 12 minutes | Serves 4

4 tablespoons butter, melted	1 tablespoon lime juice
2 cloves garlic, minced	1 teaspoon smoked paprika
Sea salt and ground black pepper, to taste	½ teaspoon onion powder
	4 salmon steaks
¼ cup dry white wine	Cooking spray

1. Place all the ingredients except the salmon and oil in a shallow dish and stir to mix well.
2. Add the salmon steaks, turning to coat well on both sides. Transfer the salmon to the refrigerator to marinate for 30 minutes.
3. Preheat the oven to 385ºF (196ºC).
4. Place the salmon steaks in the baking pan, discarding any excess marinade. Spray the salmon steaks with cooking spray.
5. Bake for about 12 minutes, flipping the salmon steaks halfway through, or until cooked to your preferred doneness.
6. Divide the salmon steaks among four plates and serve.

Honey-Glazed Cod with Sesame Seeds

Prep time: 5 minutes | Cook time: 7 to 9 minutes | Makes 1 fillet

1 tablespoon reduced-sodium soy sauce
2 teaspoons honey
Cooking spray

6 ounces (170 g) fresh cod fillet
1 teaspoon sesame seeds

1. Preheat the oven to 360ºF (182ºC).
2. In a small bowl, combine the soy sauce and honey.
3. Spray the baking pan with cooking spray, then place the cod in the pan, brush with the soy mixture, and sprinkle sesame seeds on top. Bake for 7 to 9 minutes or until opaque.
4. Remove the fish and allow to cool on a wire rack for 5 minutes before serving.

Parmesan Sriracha Tuna Patty Sliders

Prep time: 15 minutes | Cook time: 15 minutes | Serves 4

3 (5-ounce / 142-g) cans tuna, packed in water
2/3 cup whole-wheat panko bread crumbs
1/3 cup shredded Parmesan cheese

1 tablespoon sriracha
¾ teaspoon black pepper
10 whole-wheat slider buns
Cooking spray

1. Preheat the oven to 375ºF (191ºC).
2. Spray the baking pan lightly with cooking spray.
3. In a medium bowl combine the tuna, bread crumbs, Parmesan cheese, sriracha, and black pepper and stir to combine.
4. Form the mixture into 10 patties.
5. Place the patties in the pan in a single layer. Spray the patties lightly with cooking spray. You may need to cook them in batches.
6. Bake for 8 minutes. Turn the patties over and lightly spray with cooking spray. Bake until golden brown and crisp, another 7 more minutes. Serve warm.

White Fish, Carrot and Cabbage Tacos

Prep time: 10 minutes | Cook time: 15 minutes | Serves 4

1 pound (454 g) white fish fillets
2 teaspoons olive oil
3 tablespoons freshly squeezed lemon juice, divided
1½ cups chopped red cabbage

1 large carrot, grated
½ cup low-sodium salsa
1/3 cup low-fat Greek yogurt
4 soft low-sodium whole-wheat tortillas

1. Preheat the oven to 400ºF (204ºC).
2. Brush the fish with the olive oil and sprinkle with 1 tablespoon of lemon juice. Bake in the baking pan for 15 minutes, or until the fish just flakes when tested with a fork.

3. Meanwhile, in a medium bowl, stir together the remaining 2 tablespoons of lemon juice, the red cabbage, carrot, salsa, and yogurt.
4. When the fish is cooked, remove it from the pan and break it up into large pieces.
5. Offer the fish, tortillas, and the cabbage mixture, and let each person assemble a taco.
6. Serve immediately.

Salmon and Scallion Patties

Prep time: 5 minutes | Cook time: 12 minutes | Makes 6 patties

1 (14.75-ounce / 418-g) can Alaskan pink salmon, drained and bones removed
½ cup bread crumbs
1 egg, whisked

2 scallions, diced
1 teaspoon garlic powder
Salt and pepper, to taste
Cooking spray

1. Preheat the oven to 425ºF (218ºC).
2. Stir together the salmon, bread crumbs, whisked egg, scallions, garlic powder, salt, and pepper in a large bowl until well incorporated.
3. Divide the salmon mixture into six equal portions and form each into a patty with your hands.
4. Arrange the salmon patties in the baking pan and spritz them with cooking spray. Bake for 12 minutes, flipping the patties once during cooking, or until the patties are golden brown and cooked through.
5. Remove the patties from the pan and serve on a plate.

Shrimp and Artichoke Paella

Prep time: 5 minutes | Cook time: 14 to 17 minutes | Serves 4

1 (10-ounce / 284-g) package frozen cooked rice, thawed
1 (6-ounce / 170-g) jar artichoke hearts, drained and chopped
¼ cup vegetable broth

½ teaspoon dried thyme
½ teaspoon turmeric
1 cup frozen cooked small shrimp
½ cup frozen baby peas
1 tomato, diced

1. Preheat the oven to 340ºF (171ºC).
2. Mix together the cooked rice, chopped artichoke hearts, vegetable broth, thyme, and turmeric in a baking pan and stir to combine.
3. Put the baking pan in the preheated oven and bake for about 9 minutes, or until the rice is heated through.
4. Remove the pan from the oven and fold in the shrimp, baby peas, and diced tomato and mix well.
5. Return to the oven and continue cooking for 5 to 8 minutes, or until the shrimp are done and the paella is bubbling.
6. Cool for 5 minutes before serving.

Chapter 6 Poultry

Dill Chicken Strips with Italian Dressing

Prep time: 15 minutes | Cook time: 10 minutes | Serves 4

2 whole boneless, skinless chicken breasts, halved lengthwise
1 cup Italian dressing
3 cups finely crushed potato chips
1 tablespoon dried dill weed
1 tablespoon garlic powder
1 large egg, beaten
Cooking spray

1. In a large resealable bag, combine the chicken and Italian dressing. Seal the bag and refrigerate to marinate at least 1 hour.
2. In a shallow dish, stir together the potato chips, dill, and garlic powder. Place the beaten egg in a second shallow dish.
3. Remove the chicken from the marinade. Roll the chicken pieces in the egg and the potato chip mixture, coating thoroughly.
4. Preheat the oven to 325ºF (163ºC). Line the baking pan with parchment paper.
5. Place the coated chicken on the parchment and spritz with cooking spray.
6. Bake for 5 minutes. Flip the chicken, spritz it with cooking spray, and bake for 5 minutes more until the outsides are crispy and the insides are no longer pink. Serve immediately.

Ginger Chicken Thighs with Cilantro

Prep time: 10 minutes | Cook time: 10 minutes | Serves 4

¼ cup julienned peeled fresh ginger
2 tablespoons vegetable oil
1 tablespoon honey
1 tablespoon soy sauce
1 tablespoon ketchup
1 teaspoon garam masala
1 teaspoon ground turmeric
¼ teaspoon kosher salt
½ teaspoon cayenne pepper
Vegetable oil spray
1 pound (454 g) boneless, skinless chicken thighs, cut crosswise into thirds
¼ cup chopped fresh cilantro, for garnish

1. In a small bowl, combine the ginger, oil, honey, soy sauce, ketchup, garam masala, turmeric, salt, and cayenne. Whisk until well combined. Place the chicken in a resealable plastic bag and pour the marinade over. Seal the bag and massage to cover all of the chicken with the marinade. Marinate at room temperature for 30 minutes or in the refrigerator for up to 24 hours.
2. Preheat the oven to 350ºF (177ºC).
3. Spray the baking pan with vegetable oil spray and add the chicken and as much of the marinade and julienned ginger as possible. Bake for 10 minutes. Use a meat thermometer to ensure the chicken has reached an internal temperature of 165ºF (74ºC).
4. To serve, garnish with cilantro.

Chicken and Bell Pepper Fajitas

Prep time: 15 minutes | Cook time: 10 to 15 minutes | Serves 4

4 (5-ounce / 142-g) low-sodium boneless, skinless chicken breasts, cut into 4-by-½-inch strips
1 tablespoon freshly squeezed lemon juice
2 teaspoons olive oil

2 teaspoons chili powder
2 red bell peppers, sliced
4 low-sodium whole-wheat tortillas
⅓ cup nonfat sour cream
1 cup grape tomatoes, sliced

1. Preheat the oven to 380ºF (193ºC).
2. In a large bowl, mix the chicken, lemon juice, olive oil, and chili powder. Toss to coat. Transfer the chicken to the baking pan. Add the red bell peppers. Bake for 10 to 15 minutes, or until the chicken reaches an internal temperature of 165ºF (74ºC) on a meat thermometer.
3. Assemble the fajitas with the tortillas, chicken, bell peppers, sour cream, and tomatoes. Serve immediately.

Chili-Garlic Chicken Tenders

Prep time: 5 minutes | Cook time: 7 minutes | Serves 4

Seasoning:
1 teaspoon kosher salt
½ teaspoon garlic powder
½ teaspoon onion powder
½ teaspoon chili

powder
¼ teaspoon sweet paprika
¼ teaspoon freshly ground black pepper
Chicken:
8 chicken breast tenders (1 pound / 454 g total)

2 tablespoons mayonnaise

1. Preheat the oven to 400ºF (204ºC).
2. For the seasoning: In a small bowl, combine the salt, garlic powder, onion powder, chili powder, paprika, and pepper.
3. For the chicken: Place the chicken in a medium bowl and add the mayonnaise. Mix well to coat all over, then sprinkle with the seasoning mix.
4. Working in batches, arrange a single layer of the chicken in the baking pan. Bake for 7 minutes, flipping halfway, until cooked through in the center. Serve immediately.

Chicken Nuggets with Almond Crust

Prep time: 10 minutes | Cook time: 10 to 13 minutes | Serves 4

1 egg white
1 tablespoon freshly squeezed lemon juice
½ teaspoon dried basil
½ teaspoon ground paprika
1 pound (454

g) low-sodium boneless, skinless chicken breasts, cut into 1½-inch cubes
½ cup ground almonds
2 slices low-sodium whole-wheat bread, crumbled

1. Preheat the oven to 400ºF (204ºC).
2. In a shallow bowl, beat the egg white, lemon juice, basil, and paprika with a fork until foamy.
3. Add the chicken and stir to coat.
4. On a plate, mix the almonds and bread crumbs.
5. Toss the chicken cubes in the almond and bread crumb mixture until coated.
6. Bake the nuggets in the oven, in two batches, for 10 to 13 minutes, or until the chicken reaches an internal temperature of 165ºF (74ºC) on a meat thermometer. Serve immediately.

Curried Cranberry and Apple Chicken

Prep time: 12 minutes | Cook time: 18 minutes | Serves 4

3 (5-ounce / 142-g) low-sodium boneless, skinless chicken breasts, cut into 1½-inch cubes
2 teaspoons olive oil
2 tablespoons cornstarch
1 tablespoon curry powder
1 tart apple, chopped
½ cup low-sodium chicken broth
⅓ cup dried cranberries
2 tablespoons freshly squeezed orange juice
Brown rice, cooked (optional)

1. Preheat the oven to 380ºF (193ºC).
2. In a medium bowl, mix the chicken and olive oil. Sprinkle with the cornstarch and curry powder. Toss to coat. Stir in the apple and transfer to a metal pan. Bake in the oven for 8 minutes, stirring once during cooking.
3. Add the chicken broth, cranberries, and orange juice. Bake for about 10 minutes more, or until the sauce is slightly thickened and the chicken reaches an internal temperature of 165ºF (74ºC) on a meat thermometer. Serve over hot cooked brown rice, if desired.

Smoked Paprika Chicken Wings

Prep time: 15 minutes | Cook time: 24 minutes | Serves 4

1 pound (454 g) chicken wings
3 tablespoons vegetable oil
½ cup all-purpose flour
½ teaspoon smoked paprika
½ teaspoon garlic powder
½ teaspoon kosher salt
1½ teaspoons freshly cracked black pepper

1. Preheat the oven to 425ºF (218ºC).
2. Place the chicken wings in a large bowl. Drizzle the vegetable oil over wings and toss to coat.
3. In a separate bowl, whisk together the flour, paprika, garlic powder, salt, and pepper until combined.
4. Dredge the wings in the flour mixture one at a time, coating them well, and place in the baking pan. Bake for 24 minutes, turning the wings halfway through the cooking time, until the breading is browned and crunchy.
5. Serve hot.

Panko Breaded Chicken Nuggets

Prep time: 10 minutes | Cook time: 10 minutes | Serves 4

1 pound (454 g) boneless, skinless chicken breasts, cut into 1-inch pieces
2 tablespoons panko bread crumbs
6 tablespoons bread crumbs
Chicken seasoning or rub, to taste
Salt and ground black pepper, to taste
2 eggs
Cooking spray

1. Preheat the oven to 425ºF (218ºC). Spritz the baking pan with cooking spray.
2. Combine the bread crumbs, chicken seasoning, salt, and black pepper in a large bowl. Stir to mix well. Whisk the eggs in a separate bowl.
3. Dunk the chicken pieces in the egg mixture, then in the bread crumb mixture. Shake the excess off.
4. Arrange the well-coated chicken pieces in the pan. Spritz with cooking spray and bake for 10 minutes or until crispy and golden brown. You may need to work in batches to avoid overcrowding.
5. Serve immediately.

Cilantro Chicken with Lime

Prep time: 35 minutes | Cook time: 12 minutes | Serves 4

4 (4-ounce / 113-g) boneless, skinless chicken breasts	Chicken seasoning or rub, to taste
½ cup chopped fresh cilantro	Salt and ground black pepper, to taste
Juice of 1 lime	Cooking spray

1. Put the chicken breasts in the large bowl, then add the cilantro, lime juice, chicken seasoning, salt, and black pepper. Toss to coat well.
2. Wrap the bowl in plastic and refrigerate to marinate for at least 30 minutes.
3. Preheat the oven to 425ºF (218ºC). Spritz the baking pan with cooking spray.
4. Remove the marinated chicken breasts from the bowl and place in the preheated oven. Spritz with cooking spray. You may need to work in batches to avoid overcrowding.
5. Bake for 12 minutes or until the internal temperature of the chicken reaches at least 165ºF (74ºC). Flip the breasts halfway through.
6. Serve immediately.

Garlic Baked Chicken Wings

Prep time: 10 minutes | Cook time: 18 minutes | Serves 4

1 tablespoon olive oil	1 teaspoon garlic powder
8 whole chicken wings	Freshly ground black pepper, to taste
Chicken seasoning or rub, to taste	

1. Preheat the oven to 425ºF (218ºC). Grease the baking pan with olive oil.
2. On a clean work surface, rub the chicken wings with chicken seasoning and rub, garlic powder, and ground black pepper.
3. Arrange the well-coated chicken wings in the preheated oven. Bake for 18 minutes or until the internal temperature of the chicken wings reaches at least 165ºF (74ºC). Flip the chicken wings halfway through.
4. Remove the chicken wings from the oven. Serve immediately.

Turkey, Cauliflower and Onion Meatloaf

Prep time: 15 minutes | Cook time: 50 minutes | Serves 6

2 pounds (907 g) lean ground turkey	dried turmeric
1⅓ cups riced cauliflower	1 teaspoon ground cumin
2 large eggs, lightly beaten	1 teaspoon ground coriander
¼ cup almond flour	1 tablespoon minced garlic
⅔ cup chopped yellow or white onion	1 teaspoon salt
1 teaspoon ground	1 teaspoon ground black pepper
	Cooking spray

1. Preheat the oven to 350ºF (177ºC). Spritz a loaf pan with cooking spray.
2. Combine all the ingredients in a large bowl. Stir to mix well. Pour half of the mixture in the prepared loaf pan and press with a spatula to coat the bottom evenly. Spritz the mixture with cooking spray.
3. Arrange the loaf pan in the preheated oven and bake for 25 minutes or until the meat is well browned and the internal temperature reaches at least 165ºF (74ºC). Repeat with remaining mixture.
4. Remove the loaf pan from the oven and serve immediately.

Buttermilk-Marinated Chicken Breast

Prep time: 5 minutes | Cook time: 40 minutes | Serves 2

1 large bone-in, skin-on chicken breast	½ teaspoon dried dill
1 cup buttermilk	½ teaspoon onion powder
1½ teaspoons dried parsley	¼ teaspoon garlic powder
1½ teaspoons dried chives	¼ teaspoon dried tarragon
¾ teaspoon kosher salt	Cooking spray

1. Place the chicken breast in a bowl and pour over the buttermilk, turning the chicken in it to make sure it's completely covered. Let the chicken stand at room temperature for at least 20 minutes or in the refrigerator for up to 4 hours.
2. Meanwhile, in a bowl, stir together the parsley, chives, salt, dill, onion powder, garlic powder, and tarragon.
3. Preheat the oven to 300ºF (149ºC).
4. Remove the chicken from the buttermilk, letting the excess drip off, then place the chicken skin-side up directly in the oven. Sprinkle the seasoning mix all over the top of the chicken breast, then let stand until the herb mix soaks into the buttermilk, at least 5 minutes.
5. Spray the top of the chicken with cooking spray. Bake for 10 minutes, then increase the temperature to 350ºF (177ºC) and bake until an instant-read thermometer inserted into the thickest part of the breast reads 160ºF (71ºC) and the chicken is deep golden brown, 30 to 35 minutes.
6. Transfer the chicken breast to a cutting board, let rest for 10 minutes, then cut the meat off the bone and cut into thick slices for serving.

Chicken Lettuce Tacos with Peanut Sauce

Prep time: 10 minutes | Cook time: 6 minutes | Serves 4

1 pound (454 g) ground chicken	¼ cup diced onions
2 cloves garlic, minced	¼ teaspoon sea salt
	Cooking spray

Peanut Sauce:

¼ cup creamy peanut butter, at room temperature	2 tablespoons lime juice
2 tablespoons tamari	2 tablespoons grated fresh ginger
1½ teaspoons hot sauce	2 tablespoons chicken broth
	2 teaspoons sugar

For Serving:

2 small heads butter lettuce, leaves separated	Lime slices (optional)

1. Preheat the oven to 350ºF (177ºC). Spritz a baking pan with cooking spray.
2. Combine the ground chicken, garlic, and onions in the baking pan, then sprinkle with salt. Use a fork to break the ground chicken and combine them well.
3. Place the pan in the preheated oven. Bake in the preheated oven for 5 minutes or until the chicken is lightly browned. Stir them halfway through the cooking time.
4. Meanwhile, combine the ingredients for the sauce in a small bowl. Stir to mix well.
5. Pour the sauce in the pan of chicken, then cook for 1 more minute or until heated through.
6. Unfold the lettuce leaves on a large serving plate, then divide the chicken mixture on the lettuce leaves. Drizzle with lime juice and serve immediately.

BBQ Chicken Breast with Creamy Coleslaw

Prep time: 10 minutes | Cook time: 20 minutes | Serves 2

3 cups shredded coleslaw mix
Salt and pepper
2 (12-ounce / 340-g) bone-in split chicken breasts, trimmed
1 teaspoon vegetable oil
2 tablespoons barbecue sauce, plus extra for serving
2 tablespoons mayonnaise
2 tablespoons sour cream
1 teaspoon distilled white vinegar, plus extra for seasoning
¼ teaspoon sugar

1. Preheat the oven to 350ºF (177ºC).
2. Toss coleslaw mix and ¼ teaspoon salt in a colander set over bowl. Let sit until wilted slightly, about 30 minutes. Rinse, drain, and dry well with a dish towel.
3. Meanwhile, pat chicken dry with paper towels, rub with oil, and season with salt and pepper. Arrange breasts skin-side down the baking pan, spaced evenly apart, alternating ends. Bake for 10 minutes. Flip breasts and brush skin side with barbecue sauce. Return the pan to oven and bake until well browned and chicken registers 160ºF (71ºC), 10 to 15 minutes.
4. Transfer chicken to serving platter, tent loosely with aluminum foil, and let rest for 5 minutes. While chicken rests, whisk mayonnaise, sour cream, vinegar, sugar, and pinch pepper together in a large bowl. Stir in coleslaw mix and season with salt, pepper, and additional vinegar to taste. Serve chicken with coleslaw, passing extra barbecue sauce separately.

Spice-Marinated Chicken Drumsticks

Prep time: 10 minutes | Cook time: 17 minutes | Serves 4

8 (4- to 5-ounce / 113- to 142-g) skinless bone-in chicken drumsticks
½ cup plain full-fat or low-fat yogurt
¼ cup buttermilk
2 teaspoons minced garlic
2 teaspoons minced fresh ginger
2 teaspoons ground cinnamon
2 teaspoons ground coriander
2 teaspoons mild paprika
1 teaspoon salt
1 teaspoon Tabasco hot red pepper sauce

1. Preheat the oven to 400ºF (204ºC).
2. In a large bowl, stir together all the ingredients except for chicken drumsticks until well combined. Add the chicken drumsticks to the bowl and toss until well coated. Cover in plastic and set in the refrigerator to marinate for 1 hour, tossing once.
3. Arrange the marinated drumsticks in a single layer in the baking pan, leaving enough space between them. Bake for 17 minutes, or until the internal temperature of the chicken drumsticks reaches 160ºF (71ºC) on a meat thermometer. Flip the drumsticks once halfway through to ensure even cooking.
4. Transfer the drumsticks to plates. Rest for 5 minutes before serving.

Pineapple Chicken Thighs with Ginger

Prep time: 10 minutes | Cook time: 15 minutes | Serves 4

4 boneless, skinless chicken thighs (about 1½ pounds / 680 g)
1 (8-ounce / 227-g) can pineapple chunks in juice, drained, ¼ cup juice reserved
¼ cup soy sauce

¼ cup sugar
2 tablespoons ketchup
1 tablespoon minced fresh ginger
1 tablespoon minced garlic
¼ cup chopped scallions

1. Use a fork to pierce the chicken all over to allow the marinade to penetrate better. Place the chicken in a large bowl or large resealable plastic bag.
2. Set the drained pineapple chunks aside. In a small microwave-safe bowl, combine the pineapple juice, soy sauce, sugar, ketchup, ginger, and garlic. Pour half the sauce over the chicken; toss to coat. Reserve the remaining sauce. Marinate the chicken at room temperature for 30 minutes, or cover and refrigerate for up to 24 hours.
3. Preheat the oven to 350ºF (177ºC).
4. Place the chicken in the baking pan, discarding marinade. Bake for 15 minutes, turning halfway through the cooking time.
5. Meanwhile, microwave the reserved sauce on high for 45 to 60 seconds, stirring every 15 seconds, until the sauce has the consistency of a thick glaze.
6. At the end of the cooking time, use a meat thermometer to ensure the chicken has reached an internal temperature of 165ºF (74ºC).
7. Transfer the chicken to a serving platter. Pour the sauce over the chicken. Garnish with the pineapple chunks and scallions before serving.

Havarti Chicken and Ham Burgers

Prep time: 10 minutes | Cook time: 13 to 16 minutes | Serves 4

⅓ cup soft bread crumbs
3 tablespoons milk
1 egg, beaten
½ teaspoon dried thyme
Pinch salt

Freshly ground black pepper, to taste
1¼ pounds (567 g) ground chicken
¼ cup finely chopped ham
⅓ cup grated Havarti cheese
Olive oil for misting

1. Preheat the oven to 350ºF (177ºC).
2. In a medium bowl, combine the bread crumbs, milk, egg, thyme, salt, and pepper. Add the chicken and mix gently but thoroughly with clean hands.
3. Form the chicken into eight thin patties and place on waxed paper.
4. Top four of the patties with the ham and cheese. Top with remaining four patties and gently press the edges together to seal, so the ham and cheese mixture is in the middle of the burger.
5. Place the burgers in the baking pan and mist with olive oil. Bake for 13 to 16 minutes or until the chicken is thoroughly cooked to 165ºF (74ºC) as measured with a meat thermometer. Serve immediately.

Fajita Chicken Strips with Bell Peppers

Prep time: 10 minutes | Cook time: 16 minutes | Serves 4

1 pound (454 g) boneless, skinless chicken tenderloins, cut into strips
3 bell peppers, any color, cut into chunks
1 onion, cut into chunks

1 tablespoon olive oil
1 tablespoon fajita seasoning mix
Cooking spray

1. Preheat the oven to 395ºF (202ºC).
2. In a large bowl, mix together the chicken, bell peppers, onion, olive oil, and fajita seasoning mix until completely coated.
3. Spray the baking pan lightly with cooking spray.
4. Place the chicken and vegetables in the pan and lightly spray with cooking spray.
5. Bake for 8 minutes. Stir and bake for an additional 8 minutes, until the chicken is cooked through and the veggies are starting to char.
6. Serve warm.

Chicken Cordon Bleu with Swiss Cheese

Prep time: 15 minutes | Cook time: 13 to 15 minutes | Serves 4

4 chicken breast fillets
¼ cup chopped ham
$^1/_3$ cup grated Swiss or Gruyère cheese
¼ cup flour
Pinch salt

Freshly ground black pepper, to taste
½ teaspoon dried marjoram
1 egg
1 cup panko bread crumbs
Olive oil for misting

1. Preheat the oven to 380ºF (193ºC).
2. Put the chicken breast fillets on a work surface and gently press them with the palm of your hand to make them a bit thinner. Don't tear the meat.
3. In a small bowl, combine the ham and cheese. Divide this mixture among the chicken fillets. Wrap the chicken around the filling to enclose it, using toothpicks to hold the chicken together.
4. In a shallow bowl, mix the flour, salt, pepper, and marjoram. In another bowl, beat the egg. Spread the bread crumbs out on a plate.
5. Dip the chicken into the flour mixture, then into the egg, then into the bread crumbs to coat thoroughly.
6. Put the chicken in the baking pan and mist with olive oil.
7. Bake for 13 to 15 minutes or until the chicken is thoroughly cooked to 165ºF (74ºC). Carefully remove the toothpicks and serve.

Pineapple and Peach Chicken Breasts

Prep time: 10 minutes | Cook time: 14 to 15 minutes | Serves 4

1 pound (454 g) low-sodium boneless, skinless chicken breasts, cut into 1-inch pieces
1 medium red onion, chopped
1 (8-ounce / 227-g) can pineapple chunks, drained, ¼ cup juice reserved

1 tablespoon peanut oil or safflower oil
1 peach, peeled, pitted, and cubed
1 tablespoon cornstarch
½ teaspoon ground ginger
¼ teaspoon ground allspice
Brown rice, cooked (optional)

1. Preheat the oven to 380ºF (193ºC).
2. In a medium metal bowl, mix the chicken, red onion, pineapple, and peanut oil. Bake in the oven for 9 minutes. Remove and stir.
3. Add the peach and return the bowl to the oven. Bake for 3 minutes more. Remove and stir again.
4. In a small bowl, whisk the reserved pineapple juice, the cornstarch, ginger, and allspice well. Add to the chicken mixture and stir to combine.
5. Bake for 2 to 3 minutes more, or until the chicken reaches an internal temperature of 165ºF (74ºC) on a meat thermometer and the sauce is slightly thickened.
6. Serve immediately over hot cooked brown rice, if desired.

Curried Chicken with Orange and Honey

Prep time: 10 minutes | Cook time: 16 to 19 minutes | Serves 4

¾ pound (340 g) boneless, skinless chicken thighs, cut into 1-inch pieces
1 yellow bell pepper, cut into 1½-inch pieces
1 small red onion, sliced
Olive oil for misting

¼ cup chicken stock
2 tablespoons honey
¼ cup orange juice
1 tablespoon cornstarch
2 to 3 teaspoons curry powder

1. Preheat the oven to 370ºF (188ºC).
2. Put the chicken thighs, pepper, and red onion in the baking pan and mist with olive oil.
3. Bake for 12 to 14 minutes or until the chicken is cooked to 165ºF (74ºC), stirring halfway through cooking time.
4. Remove the chicken and vegetables from the oven and set aside.
5. In a metal bowl, combine the stock, honey, orange juice, cornstarch, and curry powder, and mix well. Add the chicken and vegetables, stir, and put the bowl in the oven.
6. Bake for 2 minutes. Remove and stir, then bake for 2 to 3 minutes or until the sauce is thickened and bubbly.
7. Serve warm.

Curried Cinnamon Chicken

Prep time: 5 minutes | Cook time: 18 to 23 minutes | Serves 4

²/₃ cup plain low-fat yogurt
2 tablespoons freshly squeezed lemon juice
2 teaspoons curry powder
½ teaspoon ground cinnamon

2 garlic cloves, minced
2 teaspoons olive oil
4 (5-ounce / 142-g) low-sodium boneless, skinless chicken breasts

1. In a medium bowl, whisk the yogurt, lemon juice, curry powder, cinnamon, garlic, and olive oil.
2. With a sharp knife, cut thin slashes into the chicken. Add it to the yogurt mixture and turn to coat. Let stand for 10 minutes at room temperature. You can also prepare this ahead of time and marinate the chicken in the refrigerator for up to 24 hours.
3. Preheat the oven to 360ºF (182ºC).
4. Remove the chicken from the marinade and shake off any excess liquid. Discard any remaining marinade. Place in the baking pan.
5. Bake the chicken for 10 minutes. With tongs, carefully turn each piece. Bake for 8 to 13 minutes more, or until the chicken reaches an internal temperature of 165ºF (74ºC) on a meat thermometer. Serve immediately.

Garlic Chicken Thighs with Scallions

Prep time: 10 minutes | Cook time: 30 minutes | Serves 1 to 2

2 tablespoons chicken stock
2 tablespoons reduced-sodium soy sauce
1½ tablespoons sugar
4 garlic cloves, smashed and peeled
2 large scallions, cut into 2- to 3-inch

batons, plus more, thinly sliced, for garnish
2 bone-in, skin-on chicken thighs (7 to 8 ounces / 198 to 227 g each)

1. Preheat the oven to 375ºF (191ºC).
2. In a metal cake pan, combine the chicken stock, soy sauce, and sugar and stir until the sugar dissolves. Add the garlic cloves, scallions, and chicken thighs, turning the thighs to coat them in the marinade, then resting them skin-side up. Place the pan in the oven and bake, flipping the thighs every 5 minutes after the first 10 minutes, until the chicken is cooked through and the marinade is reduced to a sticky glaze over the chicken, about 30 minutes.
3. Remove the pan from the oven and serve the chicken thighs warm, with any remaining glaze spooned over top and sprinkled with more sliced scallions.

Chicken Manchurian with Ketchup Sauce

Prep time: 10 minutes | Cook time: 20 minutes | Serves 2

1 pound (454 g) boneless, skinless chicken breasts, cut into 1-inch pieces
¼ cup ketchup
1 tablespoon tomato-based chili sauce, such as Heinz
1 tablespoon soy sauce
1 tablespoon rice vinegar

2 teaspoons vegetable oil
1 teaspoon hot sauce, such as Tabasco
½ teaspoon garlic powder
¼ teaspoon cayenne pepper
2 scallions, thinly sliced
Cooked white rice, for serving

1. Preheat the oven to 350ºF (177ºC).
2. In a bowl, combine the chicken, ketchup, chili sauce, soy sauce, vinegar, oil, hot sauce, garlic powder, cayenne, and three-quarters of the scallions and toss until evenly coated.
3. Scrape the chicken and sauce into a metal cake pan and place the pan in the oven. Bake until the chicken is cooked through and the sauce is reduced to a thick glaze, about 20 minutes, flipping the chicken pieces halfway through.
4. Remove the pan from the oven. Spoon the chicken and sauce over rice and top with the remaining scallions. Serve immediately.

Garlic Whole Chicken Bake

Prep time: 10 minutes | Cook time: 1 hour | Serves 2 to 4

½ cup melted butter
3 tablespoons garlic, minced
Salt, to taste

1 teaspoon ground black pepper
1 (1-pound / 454-g) whole chicken

1. Preheat the oven to 350ºF (177ºC).
2. Combine the butter with garlic, salt, and ground black pepper in a small bowl.
3. Brush the butter mixture over the whole chicken, then place the chicken in the preheated oven, skin side down.
4. Bake the chicken for an hour or until an instant-read thermometer inserted in the thickest part of the chicken registers at least 165ºF (74ºC). Flip the chicken halfway through.
5. Remove the chicken from the oven and allow to cool for 15 minutes before serving.

Chapter 7 Meats

Lamb Kofta with Mint

Prep time: 25 minutes | Cook time: 12 minutes | Serves 4

1 pound (454 g) ground lamb
1 tablespoon ras el hanout (North African spice)
½ teaspoon ground coriander
1 teaspoon onion powder
1 teaspoon garlic powder
1 teaspoon cumin
2 tablespoons mint, chopped
Salt and ground black pepper, to taste

Special Equipment:
4 bamboo skewers

1. Combine the ground lamb, ras el hanout, coriander, onion powder, garlic powder, cumin, mint, salt, and ground black pepper in a large bowl. Stir to mix well.
2. Transfer the mixture into sausage molds and sit the bamboo skewers in the mixture. Refrigerate for 15 minutes.
3. Preheat oven to 400ºF (204ºC). Spritz the baking pan with cooking spray.
4. Place the lamb skewers in the preheated oven and spritz with cooking spray.
5. Bake for 12 minutes or until the lamb is well browned. Flip the lamb skewers halfway through.
6. Serve immediately.

Crispy Baked Venison

Prep time: 10 minutes | Cook time: 12 minutes | Serves 4

2 eggs
¼ cup milk
1 cup whole wheat flour
½ teaspoon salt
¼ teaspoon ground
black pepper
1 pound (454 g) venison backstrap, sliced
Cooking spray

1. Preheat the oven to 385ºF (196ºC) and spritz the baking pan with cooking spray.
2. Whisk the eggs with milk in a large bowl. Combine the flour with salt and ground black pepper in a shallow dish.
3. Dredge the venison in the flour first, then into the egg mixture. Shake the excess off and roll the venison back over the flour to coat well.
4. Arrange half of the venison in the pan and spritz with cooking spray.
5. Bake for 12 minutes or until the internal temperature of the venison reaches at least 145ºF (63ºC) for medium rare. Flip the venison halfway through. Repeat with remaining venison.
6. Serve immediately.

Taco Pork Chops with Oregano

Prep time: 5 minutes | Cook time: 18 minutes | Serves 2

¼ teaspoon dried oregano
1½ teaspoons taco seasoning mix
2 (4-ounce / 113-

g) boneless pork chops
2 tablespoons unsalted butter, divided

1. Preheat the oven to 425ºF (218ºC).
2. Combine the dried oregano and taco seasoning in a small bowl and rub the mixture into the pork chops. Brush the chops with 1 tablespoon butter.
3. In the oven, bake the chops for 18 minutes, turning them over halfway through to bake on the other side.
4. When the chops are a brown color, check the internal temperature has reached 145ºF (63ºC) and remove from the oven. Serve with a garnish of remaining butter.

Miso-Sake Marinated Flank Steak

Prep time: 5 minutes | Cook time: 15 minutes | Serves 4

¾ pound (340 g) flank steak
1½ tablespoons sake
1 tablespoon brown miso paste

1 teaspoon honey
2 cloves garlic, pressed
1 tablespoon olive oil

1. Put all the ingredients in a Ziploc bag. Shake to cover the steak well with the seasonings and refrigerate for at least 1 hour.
2. Preheat the oven to 425ºF (218ºC). Coat all sides of the steak with cooking spray. Put the steak in the baking pan.
3. Bake for 15 minutes, turning the steak twice during the cooking time, then serve immediately.

Beef and Mushroom Meatloaf

Prep time: 10 minutes | Cook time: 25 minutes | Serves 4

1 pound (454 g) ground beef
1 egg, beaten
1 mushrooms, sliced
1 tablespoon thyme

1 small onion, chopped
3 tablespoons bread crumbs
Ground black pepper, to taste

1. Preheat the oven to 400ºF (204ºC).
2. Put all the ingredients into a large bowl and combine entirely.
3. Transfer the meatloaf mixture into the loaf pan.
4. Bake for 25 minutes. Slice up before serving.

Cheddar Prosciutto and Potato Salad

Prep time: 10 minutes | Cook time: 8 minutes | Serves 8

Salad:
4 pounds (1.8 kg) potatoes, boiled and cubed
15 slices prosciutto,

diced
2 cups shredded Cheddar cheese

Dressing:
15 ounces (425 g) sour cream
2 tablespoons mayonnaise
1 teaspoon salt

1 teaspoon black pepper
1 teaspoon dried basil

1. Preheat the oven to 375ºF (191ºC).
2. Put the potatoes, prosciutto, and Cheddar in a baking dish. Put it in the oven and bake for 8 minutes.
3. In a separate bowl, mix the sour cream, mayonnaise, salt, pepper, and basil using a whisk.
4. Coat the salad with the dressing and serve.

Balsamic Ribeye Steaks with Rosemary

Prep time: 10 minutes | Cook time: 18 minutes | Serves 2

¼ cup butter
1 clove garlic, minced
Salt and ground black pepper, to taste

1½ tablespoons balsamic vinegar
¼ cup rosemary, chopped
2 ribeye steaks

1. Melt the butter in a skillet over medium heat. Add the garlic and fry until fragrant.
2. Remove the skillet from the heat and add the salt, pepper, and vinegar. Allow it to cool.
3. Add the rosemary, then pour the mixture into a Ziploc bag.
4. Put the ribeye steaks in the bag and shake well, coating the meat well. Refrigerate for an hour, then allow to sit for a further twenty minutes.
5. Preheat the oven to 400ºF (204ºC).
6. Transfer the ribeye steaks to the baking pan. Bake for 18 minutes.
7. Take care when removing the steaks from the oven and plate up.
8. Serve immediately.

Smoky Beef with Jalapeño Peppers

Prep time: 10 minutes | Cook time: 45 minutes | Serves 8

2 pounds (907 g) beef, at room temperature
2 tablespoons extra-virgin olive oil
1 teaspoon sea salt flakes
1 teaspoon ground

black pepper
1 teaspoon smoked paprika
Few dashes of liquid smoke
2 jalapeño peppers, thinly sliced

1. Preheat the oven to 330ºF (166ºC).
2. With kitchen towels, pat the beef dry.
3. Massage the extra-virgin olive oil, salt, black pepper, and paprika into the meat. Cover with liquid smoke.
4. Put the beef in the oven and bake for 30 minutes. Flip the beef over and allow to bake for another 15 minutes.
5. When cooked through, serve topped with sliced jalapeños.

Beef Kofta with Cinnamon

Prep time: 10 minutes | Cook time: 13 minutes per batch | Makes 12 koftas

1½ pounds (680 g) lean ground beef
1 teaspoon onion powder
¾ teaspoon ground cinnamon
¾ teaspoon ground dried turmeric
1 teaspoon ground

cumin
¾ teaspoon salt
¼ teaspoon cayenne
12 (3½- to 4-inch-long) cinnamon sticks
Cooking spray

1. Preheat the oven to 400ºF (204ºC). Spritz the baking pan with cooking spray.
2. Combine all the ingredients, except for the cinnamon sticks, in a large bowl. Toss to mix well.
3. Divide and shape the mixture into 12 balls, then wrap each ball around each cinnamon stick and leave a quarter of the length uncovered.
4. Arrange the beef-cinnamon sticks in the pan and spritz with cooking spray. Work in batches to avoid overcrowding.
5. Bake for 15 minutes or until the beef is browned. Flip the sticks halfway through.
6. Serve immediately.

Dijon-Lemon Pork Tenderloin

Prep time: 10 minutes | Cook time: 30 minutes | Serves 4 to 6

¼ cup olive oil
¼ cup soy sauce
¼ cup freshly squeezed lemon juice
1 garlic clove, minced
1 tablespoon Dijon

mustard
1 teaspoon salt
½ teaspoon freshly ground black pepper
2 pounds (907 g) pork tenderloin

1. In a large mixing bowl, make the marinade: Mix the olive oil, soy sauce, lemon juice, minced garlic, Dijon mustard, salt, and pepper. Reserve ¼ cup of the marinade.
2. Put the tenderloin in a large bowl and pour the remaining marinade over the meat. Cover and marinate in the refrigerator for about 1 hour.
3. Preheat the oven to 400ºF (204ºC).
4. Put the marinated pork tenderloin into the baking pan. Bake for 10 minutes. Flip the pork and baste it with half of the reserved marinade. Bake for 10 minutes more.
5. Flip the pork, then baste with the remaining marinade. Bake for another 10 minutes, for a total cooking time of 30 minutes.
6. Serve immediately.

Pork and Mushroom Rolls with Teriyaki

Prep time: 10 minutes | Cook time: 10 minutes | Serves 6

4 tablespoons brown sugar
4 tablespoons mirin
4 tablespoons soy sauce
1 teaspoon almond flour

2-inch ginger, chopped
6 (4-ounce / 113-g) pork belly slices
6 ounces (170 g) Enoki mushrooms

1. Mix the brown sugar, mirin, soy sauce, almond flour, and ginger together until brown sugar dissolves.
2. Take pork belly slices and wrap around a bundle of mushrooms. Brush each roll with teriyaki sauce. Chill for half an hour.
3. Preheat the oven to 350ºF (177ºC) and add marinated pork rolls to the baking pan.
4. Bake for 10 minutes. Flip the rolls halfway through.
5. Serve immediately.

Lemongrass Pork Chops with Fish Sauce

Prep time: 15 minutes | Cook time: 15 minutes | Serves 2

1 tablespoon chopped shallot
1 tablespoon chopped garlic
1 tablespoon fish sauce
3 tablespoons lemongrass
1 teaspoon soy

sauce
1 tablespoon brown sugar
1 tablespoon olive oil
1 teaspoon ground black pepper
2 pork chops

1. Combine shallot, garlic, fish sauce, lemongrass, soy sauce, brown sugar, olive oil, and pepper in a bowl. Stir to mix well.
2. Put the pork chops in the bowl. Toss to coat well. Place the bowl in the refrigerator to marinate for 2 hours.
3. Preheat the oven to 425ºF (218ºC).
4. Remove the pork chops from the bowl and discard the marinade. Transfer the chops into the oven.
5. Bake for 15 minutes or until lightly browned. Flip the pork chops halfway through the cooking time.
6. Remove the pork chops from the oven and serve hot.

Chipotle Flank Steak with Oregano

Prep time: 5 minutes | Cook time: 18 minutes | Serves 4

3 chipotle peppers in adobo, chopped
1/3 cup chopped fresh oregano
1/3 cup chopped fresh parsley
4 cloves garlic, minced
Juice of 2 limes

1 teaspoon ground cumin seeds
1/3 cup olive oil
1 to 1½ pounds (454 g to 680 g) flank steak
Salt, to taste

1. Combine the chipotle, oregano, parsley, garlic, lime juice, cumin, and olive oil in a large bowl. Stir to mix well.
2. Dunk the flank steak in the mixture and press to coat well. Wrap the bowl in plastic and marinate under room temperature for at least 30 minutes.
3. Preheat the oven to 400°F (204°C).
4. Discard the marinade and place the steak in the preheated oven. Sprinkle with salt.
5. Bake for 18 minutes or until the steak is medium-rare or it reaches your desired doneness. Flip the steak halfway through the cooking time.
6. Remove the steak from the oven and slice to serve.

Pork Ribs with Honey-Soy Sauce

Prep time: 5 minutes | Cook time: 36 minutes | Serves 4

¼ cup soy sauce
¼ cup honey
1 teaspoon garlic powder
1 teaspoon ground dried ginger

4 (8-ounce / 227-g) boneless country-style pork ribs
Cooking spray

1. Preheat the oven to 375°F (191°C). Spritz the baking pan with cooking spray.
2. Make the teriyaki sauce: Combine the soy sauce, honey, garlic powder, and ginger in a bowl. Stir to mix well.
3. Brush the ribs with half of the teriyaki sauce, then arrange the ribs in the pan. Spritz with cooking spray. You may need to work in batches to avoid overcrowding.
4. Bake for 36 minutes or until the internal temperature of the ribs reaches at least 145°F (63°C). Brush the ribs with remaining teriyaki sauce and flip halfway through.
5. Serve immediately.

Dijon Mustard Pork Tenderloin

Prep time: 5 minutes | Cook time: 12 minutes | Serves 6

2 large egg whites
1½ tablespoons Dijon mustard
2 cups crushed pretzel crumbs

1½ pounds (680 g) pork tenderloin, cut into ¼-pound (113-g) sections
Cooking spray

1. Preheat the oven to 375ºF (191ºC). Spritz the baking pan with cooking spray.
2. Whisk the egg whites with Dijon mustard in a bowl until bubbly. Pour the pretzel crumbs in a separate bowl.
3. Dredge the pork tenderloin in the egg white mixture and press to coat. Shake the excess off and roll the tenderloin over the pretzel crumbs.
4. Arrange the well-coated pork tenderloin in batches in a single layer in the pan and spritz with cooking spray.
5. Bake for 12 minutes or until the pork is golden brown and crispy. Flip the pork halfway through. Repeat with remaining pork sections.
6. Serve immediately.

Beef Stroganoff with Mushrooms

Prep time: 15 minutes | Cook time: 17 minutes | Serves 4

1 pound (454 g) beef steak, thinly sliced
8 ounces (227 g) mushrooms, sliced
1 whole onion, chopped
2 cups beef broth

1 cup sour cream
4 tablespoons butter, melted
2 cups cooked egg noodles

1. Preheat the oven to 425ºF (218ºC).
2. Combine the mushrooms, onion, beef broth, sour cream and butter in a bowl until well blended. Add the beef steak to another bowl.
3. Spread the mushroom mixture over the steak and let marinate for 10 minutes.
4. Pour the marinated steak in a baking pan and bake in the preheated oven for 17 minutes, or until the steak is browned and the vegetables are tender.
5. Serve hot with the cooked egg noodles.

Beef Meatloaf with Tomato Sauce

Prep time: 15 minutes | Cook time: 25 minutes | Serves 4

1½ pounds (680 g) ground beef
1 cup tomato sauce
½ cup bread crumbs
2 egg whites
½ cup grated Parmesan cheese
1 diced onion
2 tablespoons chopped parsley

2 tablespoons minced ginger
2 garlic cloves, minced
½ teaspoon dried basil
1 teaspoon cayenne pepper
Salt and ground black pepper, to taste
Cooking spray

1. Preheat the oven to 360ºF (182ºC). Spritz a meatloaf pan with cooking spray.
2. Combine all the ingredients in a large bowl. Stir to mix well.
3. Pour the meat mixture in the prepared meatloaf pan and press with a spatula to make it firm.
4. Arrange the pan in the preheated oven and bake for 25 minutes or until the beef is well browned.
5. Serve immediately.

Orange Pork Ribs with Garlic

Prep time: 1 hour 10 minutes | Cook time: 30 minutes | Serves 6

2½ pounds (1.1 kg) boneless country-style pork ribs, cut into 2-inch pieces
3 tablespoons olive brine
1 tablespoon minced fresh oregano leaves
1/3 cup orange juice

1 teaspoon ground cumin
1 tablespoon minced garlic
1 teaspoon salt
1 teaspoon ground black pepper
Cooking spray

1. Combine all the ingredients in a large bowl. Toss to coat the pork ribs well. Wrap the bowl in plastic and refrigerate for at least an hour to marinate.
2. Preheat the oven to 425°F (218°C) and spritz the baking pan with cooking spray.
3. Arrange the marinated pork ribs in a single layer in the pan and spritz with cooking spray.
4. Bake for 30 minutes or until well browned. Flip the ribs halfway through.
5. Serve immediately.

Beef, Kale and Tomato Omelet

Prep time: 15 minutes | Cook time: 18 minutes | Serves 4

½ pound (227 g) leftover beef, coarsely chopped
2 garlic cloves, pressed
1 cup kale, torn into pieces and wilted
1 tomato, chopped
¼ teaspoon sugar

4 eggs, beaten
4 tablespoons heavy cream
½ teaspoon turmeric powder
Salt and ground black pepper, to taste
⅛ teaspoon ground allspice
Cooking spray

1. Preheat the oven to 385°F (196°C). Spritz four ramekins with cooking spray.
2. Put equal amounts of each of the ingredients into each ramekin and mix well.
3. Bake for 18 minutes. Serve immediately.

BBQ Sausage with Pineapple and Bell Peppers

Prep time: 15 minutes | Cook time: 12 minutes | Serves 2 to 4

¾ pound (340 g) kielbasa sausage, cut into ½-inch slices
1 (8-ounce / 227-g) can pineapple chunks in juice, drained

1 cup bell pepper chunks
1 tablespoon barbecue seasoning
1 tablespoon soy sauce
Cooking spray

1. Preheat the oven to 425°F (218°C). Spritz the baking pan with cooking spray.
2. Combine all the ingredients in a large bowl. Toss to mix well.
3. Pour the sausage mixture in the preheated oven.
4. Bake for 12 minutes or until the sausage is lightly browned and the bell pepper and pineapple are soft.
5. Serve immediately.

Panko Breaded Wasabi Spam

Prep time: 5 minutes | Cook time: 12 minutes | Serves 3

²/₃ cup all-purpose flour
2 large eggs
1½ tablespoons wasabi paste

2 cups panko bread crumbs
6½-inch-thick spam slices
Cooking spray

1. Preheat the oven to 425ºF (218ºC) and spritz the baking pan with cooking spray.
2. Pour the flour in a shallow plate. Whisk the eggs with wasabi in a large bowl. Pour the panko in a separate shallow plate.

3. Dredge the spam slices in the flour first, then dunk in the egg mixture, and then roll the spam over the panko to coat well. Shake the excess off.
4. Arrange the spam slices in a single layer in the pan and spritz with cooking spray.
5. Bake for 15 minutes or until the spam slices are golden and crispy. Flip the spam slices halfway through.
6. Serve immediately.

Beef and Spaghetti Squash Lasagna

Prep time: 5 minutes | Cook time: 1 hour 15 minutes | Serves 6

2 large spaghetti squash, cooked (about 2¾ pounds / 1.2 kg)
4 pounds (1.8 kg) ground beef
1 (2½-pound / 1.1-kg) large jar Marinara

sauce
25 slices Mozzarella cheese
30 ounces whole-milk ricotta cheese

1. Preheat the oven to 375ºF (191ºC).
2. Slice the spaghetti squash and place it face down inside a baking dish. Fill with water until covered.
3. Bake in the preheated oven for 45 minutes until skin is soft.
4. Sear the ground beef in a skillet over medium-high heat for 5 minutes or until browned, then add the marinara sauce and heat until warm. Set aside.
5. Scrape the flesh off the cooked squash to resemble strands of spaghetti.
6. Layer the lasagna in a large greased pan in alternating layers of spaghetti squash, beef sauce, Mozzarella, ricotta. Repeat until all the ingredients have been used.
7. Bake for 30 minutes and serve!

Paprika Lamb Chops with Sage

Prep time: 5 minutes | Cook time: 30 minutes | Serves 4

1 cup all-purpose flour
2 teaspoons dried sage leaves
2 teaspoons garlic powder
1 tablespoon mild paprika

1 tablespoon salt
4 (6-ounce / 170-g) bone-in lamb shoulder chops, fat trimmed
Cooking spray

1. Preheat the oven to 400°F (204°C) and spritz the baking pan with cooking spray.
2. Combine the flour, sage leaves, garlic powder, paprika, and salt in a large bowl. Stir to mix well. Dunk in the lamb chops and toss to coat well.
3. Arrange the lamb chops in a single layer in the pan and spritz with cooking spray. Bake for 30 minutes or until the chops are golden brown and reaches your desired doneness. Flip the chops halfway through.
4. Serve immediately.

Dill-Thyme Beef Steak

Prep time: 5 minutes | Cook time: 26 minutes | Serves 6

1 teaspoon dried dill
1 teaspoon dried thyme
1 teaspoon garlic powder

2 pounds (907 g) beef steak
3 tablespoons butter

1. Preheat the oven to 385°F (196°C).
2. Combine the dill, thyme, and garlic powder in a small bowl, and massage into the steak.
3. Bake the steak in the oven for 24 minutes, then remove, shred, and return to the oven.
4. Add the butter and bake the shredded steak for a further 2 minutes at 365°F (185°C). Make sure the beef is coated in the butter before serving.

Beef and Carrot Meatballs

Prep time: 10 minutes | Cook time: 14 minutes | Serves 8

1 pound (454 g) ground beef
1 egg, beaten
2 carrots, shredded
2 bread slices, crumbled
1 small onion, minced

½ teaspoons garlic salt
Pepper and salt, to taste
1 cup tomato sauce
2 cups pasta sauce

1. Preheat the oven to 425°F (218°C).
2. In a bowl, combine the ground beef, egg, carrots, crumbled bread, onion, garlic salt, pepper and salt.
3. Divide the mixture into equal amounts and shape each one into a small meatball.
4. Put them in the baking pan and bake for 8 minutes.
5. Transfer the meatballs to an oven-safe dish and top with the tomato sauce and pasta sauce.
6. Set the dish into the oven and allow to bake at 350°F (177°C) for 6 more minutes. Serve hot.

Chapter 8 Appetizers and Snacks

Ricotta Phyllo Artichoke Triangles

Prep time: 15 minutes | Cook time: 9 to 12 minutes | Makes 18 triangles

¼ cup Ricotta cheese
1 egg white
⅓ cup minced and drained artichoke hearts
3 tablespoons grated Mozzarella cheese
½ teaspoon dried thyme
6 sheets frozen phyllo dough, thawed
2 tablespoons melted butter

1. Preheat the oven to 400ºF (204ºC).
2. In a small bowl, combine the Ricotta cheese, egg white, artichoke hearts, Mozzarella cheese, and thyme, and mix well.
3. Cover the phyllo dough with a damp kitchen towel while you work so it doesn't dry out. Using one sheet at a time, place on the work surface and cut into thirds lengthwise.
4. Put about 1½ teaspoons of the filling on each strip at the base. Fold the bottom right-hand tip of phyllo over the filling to meet the other side in a triangle, then continue folding in a triangle. Brush each triangle with butter to seal the edges. Repeat with the remaining phyllo dough and filling.
5. Place the triangles in the baking pan. Bake, 6 at a time, for about 3 to 4 minutes, or until the phyllo is golden brown and crisp.
6. Serve hot.

Chili Kale Chips with Sesame Seeds

Prep time: 15 minutes | Cook time: 10 minutes | Serves 5

8 cups deribbed kale leaves, torn into 2-inch pieces
1½ tablespoons olive oil
¾ teaspoon chili powder
¼ teaspoon garlic powder
½ teaspoon paprika
2 teaspoons sesame seeds

1. Preheat oven to 375ºF (191ºC).
2. In a large bowl, toss the kale with the olive oil, chili powder, garlic powder, paprika, and sesame seeds until well coated.
3. Put the kale in the baking pan and bake for 10 minutes, flipping the kale twice during cooking, or until the kale is crispy.
4. Serve warm.

Baked Bacon-Wrapped Dates

Prep time: 10 minutes | Cook time: 10 to 14 minutes | Serves 6

12 dates, pitted
6 slices high-quality bacon, cut in half
Cooking spray

1. Preheat the oven to 360ºF (182ºC).
2. Wrap each date with half a bacon slice and secure with a toothpick.
3. Spray the baking pan with cooking spray, then place 6 bacon-wrapped dates in the pan and bake for 5 to 7 minutes or until the bacon is crispy. Repeat this process with the remaining dates.
4. Remove the dates and allow to cool on a wire rack for 5 minutes before serving.

Parmesan Cauliflower with Turmeric

Prep time: 15 minutes | Cook time: 15 minutes | Makes 5 cups

8 cups small cauliflower florets (about 1¼ pounds / 567 g)
3 tablespoons olive oil
1 teaspoon garlic powder
½ teaspoon salt
½ teaspoon turmeric
¼ cup shredded Parmesan cheese

1. Preheat the oven to 425ºF (218ºC).
2. In a bowl, combine the cauliflower florets, olive oil, garlic powder, salt, and turmeric and toss to coat.
3. Transfer to the baking and bake for 18 minutes, or until the florets are crisp-tender.
4. Remove from the pan to a plate. Sprinkle with the shredded Parmesan cheese and toss well. Serve warm.

Cinnamon Nut Mix

Prep time: 5 minutes | Cook time: 20 minutes | Serves 6

2 cups mixed nuts (walnuts, pecans, and almonds)
2 tablespoons egg white
2 tablespoons sugar
1 teaspoon paprika
1 teaspoon ground cinnamon
Cooking spray

1. Preheat the oven to 300ºF (149ºC). Spray the baking pan with cooking spray.
2. Stir together the mixed nuts, egg white, sugar, paprika, and cinnamon in a small bowl until the nuts are fully coated.
3. Put the nuts in the pan and bake for 20 minutes. Stir halfway through the cooking time for even cooking.
4. Transfer the nuts to a bowl and serve warm.

Cinnamon Apple Chips

Prep time: 10 minutes | Cook time: 12 minutes | Serves 4

4 medium apples (any type will work), cored and thinly sliced
¼ teaspoon nutmeg
¼ teaspoon cinnamon
Cooking spray

1. Preheat oven to 385ºF (196ºC).
2. Place the apple slices in a large bowl and sprinkle the spices on top. Toss to coat.
3. Working in batches, place the apple slices in the baking pan in a single layer and spray them with cooking spray.
4. Bake for 12 minutes, or until the apple chips are crispy.
5. Transfer the apple chips to a paper towel-lined plate and rest for 5 minutes before serving.

Almond-Stuffed Dates with Turkey Bacon

Prep time: 10 minutes | Cook time: 8 minutes | Makes 16 appetizers

16 whole dates, pitted
16 whole almonds
6 to 8 strips turkey bacon, cut in half

Special Equipment:
16 toothpicks, soaked in water for at least 30 minutes

1. Preheat the oven to 400ºF (204ºC).
2. On a flat work surface, stuff each pitted date with a whole almond.
3. Wrap half slice of bacon around each date and secure it with a toothpick.
4. Place the bacon-wrapped dates in the baking pan and bake for 8 minutes, or until the bacon is cooked to your desired crispiness.
5. Transfer the dates to a paper towel-lined plate to drain. Serve hot.

Paprika-Mustard Pork Spareribs

Prep time: 5 minutes | Cook time: 35 minutes | Serves 2

1 tablespoon kosher salt
1 tablespoon dark brown sugar
1 tablespoon sweet paprika
1 teaspoon garlic powder
1 teaspoon onion powder
1 teaspoon poultry seasoning
½ teaspoon mustard powder
½ teaspoon freshly ground black pepper
2¼ pounds (1 kg) individually cut St. Louis–style pork spareribs

1. Preheat the oven to 350°F (177°C).
2. In a large bowl, whisk together the salt, brown sugar, paprika, garlic powder, onion powder, poultry seasoning, mustard powder, and pepper. Add the ribs and toss. Rub the seasonings into them with your hands until they're fully coated.
3. Arrange the ribs in the baking pan. Bake for 35 minutes, or until the ribs are tender inside and golden brown and crisp on the outside. Transfer the ribs to plates and serve hot.

Cayenne Mixed Nuts with Sesame Seeds

Prep time: 10 minutes | Cook time: 2 minutes | Makes 4 cups

1 tablespoon buttery spread, melted
2 teaspoons honey
¼ teaspoon cayenne pepper
2 teaspoons sesame seeds
¼ teaspoon kosher salt
¼ teaspoon freshly ground black pepper
1 cup cashews
1 cup almonds
1 cup mini pretzels
1 cup rice squares cereal
Cooking spray

1. Preheat the oven to 360°F (182°C).
2. In a large bowl, combine the buttery spread, honey, cayenne pepper, sesame seeds, kosher salt, and black pepper, then add the cashews, almonds, pretzels, and rice squares, tossing to coat.
3. Spray a baking pan with cooking spray, then pour the mixture into the pan and bake for 2 minutes.
4. Remove the sesame mix from the oven and allow to cool in the pan on a wire rack for 5 minutes before serving.

Cheddar Sausage Balls

Prep time: 10 minutes | Cook time: 10 to 11 minutes | Serves 8

12 ounces (340 g) mild ground sausage
1½ cups baking mix
1 cup shredded mild Cheddar cheese
3 ounces (85 g) cream cheese, at room temperature
1 to 2 tablespoons olive oil

1. Preheat the oven to 325°F (163°C). Line the baking pan with parchment paper.
2. Mix together the ground sausage, baking mix, Cheddar cheese, and cream cheese in a large bowl and stir to incorporate.
3. Divide the sausage mixture into 16 equal portions and roll them into 1-inch balls with your hands.
4. Arrange the sausage balls on the parchment, leaving space between each ball. You may need to work in batches to avoid overcrowding.
5. Brush the sausage balls with the olive oil. Bake for 10 to 11 minutes, or until the balls are firm and lightly browned on both sides.
6. Remove from the pan to a plate and repeat with the remaining balls.
7. Serve warm.

Prosciutto-Wrapped Asparagus Spears

Prep time: 5 minutes | Cook time: 5 minutes | Serves 6

12 asparagus spears, woody ends trimmed   Cooking spray
24 pieces thinly sliced prosciutto

1. Preheat the oven to 380ºF (193ºC).
2. Wrap each asparagus spear with 2 slices of prosciutto, then repeat this process with the remaining asparagus and prosciutto.
3. Spray the baking pan with cooking spray, then place 2 to 3 bundles in the pan and bake for 5 minutes. Repeat this process with the remaining asparagus bundles.
4. Remove the bundles and allow to cool on a wire rack for 5 minutes before serving.

Apple Chips

Prep time: 5 minutes | Cook time: 35 minutes | Serves 1

1 Honeycrisp or Pink Lady apple

1. Preheat the oven to 325ºF (163ºC).
2. Core the apple with an apple corer, leaving apple whole. Cut the apple into ⅛-inch-thick slices.
3. Arrange the apple slices in the baking pan, staggering slices as much as possible. Bake for 35 minutes, or until the chips are dry and some are lightly browned, turning 4 times with tongs to separate and rotate them from top to bottom.
4. Place the chips in a single layer on a wire rack to cool. Apples will become crisper as they cool. Serve immediately.

Mozzarella Hash Brown Bruschetta

Prep time: 5 minutes | Cook time: 6 to 8 minutes | Serves 4

4 frozen hash brown patties
1 tablespoon olive oil
⅓ cup chopped cherry tomatoes
3 tablespoons diced fresh Mozzarella

2 tablespoons grated Parmesan cheese
1 tablespoon balsamic vinegar
1 tablespoon minced fresh basil

1. Preheat the oven to 425ºF (218ºC).
2. Place the hash brown patties in the baking pan in a single layer. Bake for 8 minutes, or until the potatoes are crisp, hot, and golden brown.
3. Meanwhile, combine the olive oil, tomatoes, Mozzarella, Parmesan, vinegar, and basil in a small bowl.
4. When the potatoes are done, carefully remove from the pan and arrange on a serving plate. Top with the tomato mixture and serve.

Beef Cubes with Cheese Pasta Sauce

Prep time: 10 minutes | Cook time: 12 to 16 minutes | Serves 4

1 pound (454 g) sirloin tip, cut into 1-inch cubes
1 cup cheese pasta sauce

1½ cups soft bread crumbs
2 tablespoons olive oil
½ teaspoon dried marjoram

1. Preheat the oven to 380ºF (193ºC).
2. In a medium bowl, toss the beef with the pasta sauce to coat.
3. In a shallow bowl, combine the bread crumbs, oil, and marjoram, and mix well. Drop the beef cubes, one at a time, into the bread crumb mixture to coat thoroughly. Transfer to the baking pan.
4. Bake the beef in two batches for 10 minutes, or until the beef is at least 145ºF (63ºC) and the outside is crisp and brown.
5. Serve hot.

Balsamic Mango and Beef Skewers

Prep time: 10 minutes | Cook time: 4 to 7 minutes | Serves 4

¾ pound (340 g) beef sirloin tip, cut into 1-inch cubes
2 tablespoons balsamic vinegar
1 tablespoon olive oil
1 tablespoon honey

½ teaspoon dried marjoram
Pinch of salt
Freshly ground black pepper, to taste
1 mango

1. Preheat the oven to 390ºF (199ºC).
2. Put the beef cubes in a medium bowl and add the balsamic vinegar, olive oil, honey, marjoram, salt, and pepper. Mix well, then massage the marinade into the beef with your hands. Set aside.
3. To prepare the mango, stand it on end and cut the skin off, using a sharp knife. Then carefully cut around the oval pit to remove the flesh. Cut the mango into 1-inch cubes.
4. Thread metal skewers alternating with three beef cubes and two mango cubes.
5. Bake the skewers in the oven for 4 to 7 minutes, or until the beef is browned and at least 145ºF (63ºC).
6. Serve hot.

Garlic-Paprika Potato Chips

Prep time: 5 minutes | Cook time: 25 minutes | Serves 3

2 medium potatoes, preferably Yukon Gold, scrubbed
Cooking spray
2 teaspoons olive oil
½ teaspoon garlic granules

¼ teaspoon paprika
¼ teaspoon plus ⅛ teaspoon sea salt
¼ teaspoon freshly ground black pepper
Ketchup or hot sauce, for serving

1. Preheat the oven to 425ºF (218ºC). Spritz the baking pan with cooking spray.
2. On a flat work surface, cut the potatoes into ¼-inch-thick slices. Transfer the potato slices to a medium bowl, along with the olive oil, garlic granules, paprika, salt, and pepper and toss to coat well.
3. Put the potato slices in the pan and bake for 25 minutes until tender and nicely browned.
4. Remove from the pan and serve alongside the ketchup for dipping.

Cheesy Salsa Stuffed Mushrooms

Prep time: 10 minutes | Cook time: 15 minutes | Serves 4

16 medium button mushrooms, rinsed and patted dry
¹⁄₃ cup low-sodium salsa
3 garlic cloves, minced
1 medium onion, finely chopped

1 jalapeño pepper, minced
⅛ teaspoon cayenne pepper
3 tablespoons shredded Pepper Jack cheese
2 teaspoons olive oil

1. Preheat the oven to 375ºF (191ºC).
2. Remove the stems from the mushrooms and finely chop them, reserving the whole caps.
3. In a medium bowl, mix the salsa, garlic, onion, jalapeño, cayenne, and Pepper Jack cheese. Stir in the chopped mushroom stems.
4. Stuff this mixture into the mushroom caps, mounding the filling. Drizzle the olive oil on the mushrooms. Bake the mushrooms in the baking pan for 15 minutes, or until the filling is hot and the mushrooms are tender.
5. Serve immediately.

Mozzarella Bruschetta with Basil Pesto

Prep time: 10 minutes | Cook time: 5 to 11 minutes | Serves 4

8 slices French bread, ½ inch thick
2 tablespoons softened butter
1 cup shredded Mozzarella cheese

½ cup basil pesto
1 cup chopped grape tomatoes
2 green onions, thinly sliced

1. Preheat the oven to 350ºF (177ºC).
2. Spread the bread with the butter and place butter-side up in the baking pan. Bake for 3 to 5 minutes, or until the bread is light golden brown.
3. Remove the bread from the pan and top each piece with some of the cheese. Return to the pan in 2 batches and bake for 1 to 3 minutes, or until the cheese melts.
4. Meanwhile, combine the pesto, tomatoes, and green onions in a small bowl.
5. When the cheese has melted, remove the bread from the oven and place on a serving plate. Top each slice with some of the pesto mixture and serve.

Paprika Deviled Eggs with Dill Pickle

Prep time: 20 minutes | Cook time: 16 minutes | Serves 12

3 cups ice
12 large eggs
½ cup mayonnaise
10 hamburger dill pickle chips, diced
¼ cup diced onion

2 teaspoons salt
2 teaspoons yellow mustard
1 teaspoon freshly ground black pepper
½ teaspoon paprika

1. Preheat the oven to 250°F (121°C).
2. Put the ice in a large bowl.
3. Place the eggs in the baking pan and bake for 16 minutes.
4. Remove the eggs from the pan to the large bowl of ice to cool.
5. When cool enough to handle, peel the eggs. Slice them in half lengthwise and scoop out yolks into a small bowl. Stir in the mayonnaise, pickles, onion, salt, mustard, and pepper. Mash the mixture with a fork until well combined.
6. Fill each egg white half with 1 to 2 teaspoons of the egg yolk mixture.
7. Sprinkle the paprika on top and serve immediately.

Broccoli, Spinach and Bell Pepper Dip

Prep time: 10 minutes | Cook time: 9 to 14 minutes | Serves 4

½ cup low-fat Greek yogurt
¼ cup nonfat cream cheese
½ cup frozen chopped broccoli, thawed and drained
½ cup frozen chopped spinach, thawed and drained

$1/_3$ cup chopped red bell pepper
1 garlic clove, minced
½ teaspoon dried oregano
2 tablespoons grated low-sodium Parmesan cheese

1. Preheat the oven to 340°F (171°C).
2. In a medium bowl, blend the yogurt and cream cheese until well combined.
3. Stir in the broccoli, spinach, red bell pepper, garlic, and oregano. Transfer to a baking pan. Sprinkle with the Parmesan cheese.
4. Place the pan in the oven. Bake for 9 to 14 minutes, or until the dip is bubbly and the top starts to brown.
5. Serve immediately.

Chapter 9 Desserts

Graham Cracker Chocolate Cheesecake

Prep time: 10 minutes | Cook time: 20 minutes | Serves 8

1 cup graham cracker crumbs
3 tablespoons softened butter
1½ (8-ounce / 227-g) packages cream cheese, softened
⅓ cup sugar
2 eggs
1 tablespoon flour
1 teaspoon vanilla
¼ cup chocolate syrup

1. For the crust, combine the graham cracker crumbs and butter in a small bowl and mix well. Press into the bottom of a baking pan and put in the freezer to set.
2. For the filling, combine the cream cheese and sugar in a medium bowl and mix well. Beat in the eggs, one at a time. Add the flour and vanilla.
3. Preheat the oven to 450ºF (232ºC).
4. Remove ⅔ cup of the filling to a small bowl and stir in the chocolate syrup until combined.
5. Pour the vanilla filling into the pan with the crust. Drop the chocolate filling over the vanilla filling by the spoonful. With a clean butter knife, stir the fillings in a zigzag pattern to marbleize them.
6. Bake for 20 minutes or until the cheesecake is just set.
7. Cool on a wire rack for 1 hour, then chill in the refrigerator until the cheesecake is firm.
8. Serve immediately.

Vanilla Chocolate Cookie

Prep time: 10 minutes | Cook time: 9 minutes | Serves 4

Nonstick baking spray with flour
3 tablespoons softened butter
⅓ cup plus 1 tablespoon brown sugar
1 egg yolk
½ cup flour
2 tablespoons ground white chocolate
¼ teaspoon baking soda
½ teaspoon vanilla
¾ cup chocolate chips

1. Preheat the oven to 350ºF (177ºC).
2. In a medium bowl, beat the butter and brown sugar together until fluffy. Stir in the egg yolk.
3. Add the flour, white chocolate, baking soda, and vanilla, and mix well. Stir in the chocolate chips.
4. Line a baking pan with parchment paper. Spray the parchment paper with nonstick baking spray with flour.
5. Spread the batter into the prepared pan, leaving a ½-inch border on all sides.
6. Bake for about 9 minutes or until the cookie is light brown and just barely set.
7. Remove the pan from the oven and let cool for 10 minutes. Remove the cookie from the pan, remove the parchment paper, and let cool on a wire rack.
8. Serve immediately.

Honey-Glazed Pears with Walnuts

Prep time: 5 minutes | Cook time: 20 minutes | Serves 4

2 large Bosc pears, halved and deseeded
3 tablespoons honey
1 tablespoon unsalted butter

½ teaspoon ground cinnamon
¼ cup walnuts, chopped
¼ cup part skim low-fat ricotta cheese, divided

1. Preheat the oven to 350ºF (177ºC).
2. In a baking pan, place the pears, cut side up.
3. In a small microwave-safe bowl, melt the honey, butter, and cinnamon. Brush this mixture over the cut sides of the pears.
4. Pour 3 tablespoons of water around the pears in the pan. Bake the pears for 20 minutes, or until tender when pierced with a fork and slightly crisp on the edges, basting once with the liquid in the pan.
5. Carefully remove the pears from the pan and place on a serving plate. Drizzle each with some liquid from the pan, sprinkle the walnuts on top, and serve with a spoonful of ricotta cheese.

Raisin Oatmeal Bars

Prep time: 15 minutes | Cook time: 15 minutes | Serves 8

¹/₃ cup all-purpose flour
¼ teaspoon kosher salt
¼ teaspoon baking powder
¼ teaspoon ground cinnamon
¼ cup light brown sugar, lightly

packed
¼ cup granulated sugar
½ cup canola oil
1 large egg
1 teaspoon vanilla extract
1¹/₃ cups quick-cooking oats
¹/₃ cup raisins

1. Preheat the oven to 360ºF (182ºC).
2. In a large bowl, combine the all-purpose flour, kosher salt, baking powder, ground cinnamon, light brown sugar, granulated sugar, canola oil, egg, vanilla extract, quick-cooking oats, and raisins.
3. Spray a baking pan with nonstick cooking spray, then pour the oat mixture into the pan and press down to evenly distribute. Place the pan in the oven and bake for 15 minutes or until golden brown.
4. Remove from the oven and allow to cool in the pan on a wire rack for 20 minutes before slicing and serving.

Apple and Pear Crisp with Walnuts

Prep time: 10 minutes | Cook time: 20 minutes | Serves 6

½ pound (227 g) apples, cored and chopped
½ pound (227 g) pears, cored and chopped
1 cup flour
1 cup sugar
1 tablespoon butter
1 teaspoon ground

cinnamon
¼ teaspoon ground cloves
1 teaspoon vanilla extract
¼ cup chopped walnuts
Whipped cream, for serving

1. Preheat the oven to 340ºF (171ºC).
2. Lightly grease a baking dish and place the apples and pears inside.
3. Combine the rest of the ingredients, minus the walnuts and the whipped cream, until a coarse, crumbly texture is achieved.
4. Pour the mixture over the fruits and spread it evenly. Top with the chopped walnuts.
5. Bake for 20 minutes or until the top turns golden brown.
6. Serve at room temperature with whipped cream.

Brown Sugar-Lemon Applesauce

Prep time: 10 minutes | Cook time: 1 hour | Makes 1¼ cups

Cooking spray
2 cups unsweetened applesauce
⅔ cup packed light brown sugar
3 tablespoons fresh lemon juice
½ teaspoon kosher salt
¼ teaspoon ground cinnamon
⅛ teaspoon ground allspice

1. Preheat the oven to 340°F (171°C).
2. Spray a metal cake pan with cooking spray. Whisk together all the ingredients in a bowl until smooth, then pour into the greased pan. Set the pan in the oven and bake until the apple mixture is caramelized, reduced to a thick purée, and fragrant, about 1 hour.
3. Remove the pan from the oven, stir to combine the caramelized bits at the edge with the rest, then let cool completely to thicken.
4. Serve immediately.

Lemon Blackberry and Granola Crisp

Prep time: 5 minutes | Cook time: 20 minutes | Serves 1

2 tablespoons lemon juice
⅓ cup powdered erythritol
¼ teaspoon
xantham gum
2 cup blackberries
1 cup crunchy granola

1. Preheat the oven to 350°F (177°C).
2. In a bowl, combine the lemon juice, erythritol, xantham gum, and blackberries. Transfer to a round baking dish and cover with aluminum foil.
3. Put the dish in the oven and bake for 12 minutes.

4. Take care when removing the dish from the oven. Give the blackberries a stir and top with the granola.
5. Return the dish to the oven and bake for an additional 3 minutes, this time at 320°F (160°C). Serve once the granola has turned brown and enjoy.

Orange Cornmeal Cake

Prep time: 10 minutes | Cook time: 23 minutes | Serves 8

Nonstick baking spray with flour
1¼ cups all-purpose flour
⅓ cup yellow cornmeal
¾ cup white sugar
1 teaspoon baking
soda
¼ cup safflower oil
1¼ cups orange juice, divided
1 teaspoon vanilla
¼ cup powdered sugar

1. Preheat the oven to 350°F (177°C).
2. Spray a baking pan with nonstick spray and set aside.
3. In a medium bowl, combine the flour, cornmeal, sugar, baking soda, safflower oil, 1 cup of the orange juice, and vanilla, and mix well.
4. Pour the batter into the baking pan and place in the oven. Bake for 23 minutes or until a toothpick inserted in the center of the cake comes out clean.
5. Remove the cake from the oven and place on a cooling rack. Using a toothpick, make about 20 holes in the cake.
6. In a small bowl, combine remaining ¼ cup of orange juice and the powdered sugar and stir well. Drizzle this mixture over the hot cake slowly so the cake absorbs it.
7. Cool completely, then cut into wedges to serve.

Vanilla Peaches with Fresh Blueberries

Prep time: 10 minutes | Cook time: 7 to 11 minutes | Serves 6

3 peaches, peeled, halved, and pitted
2 tablespoons packed brown sugar
1 cup plain Greek yogurt
¼ teaspoon ground cinnamon
1 teaspoon pure vanilla extract
1 cup fresh blueberries

1. Preheat the oven to 380ºF (193ºC).
2. Arrange the peaches in the baking pan, cut-side up. Top with a generous sprinkle of brown sugar.
3. Bake in the preheated oven for 7 to 11 minutes, or until the peaches are lightly browned and caramelized.
4. Meanwhile, whisk together the yogurt, cinnamon, and vanilla in a small bowl until smooth.
5. Remove the peaches from the pan to a plate. Serve topped with the yogurt mixture and fresh blueberries.

Vanilla Chocolate Brownies

Prep time: 10 minutes | Cook time: 20 minutes | Makes 1 dozen brownies

1 egg
¼ cup brown sugar
2 tablespoons white sugar
2 tablespoons safflower oil
1 teaspoon vanilla
1/3 cup all-purpose
flour
¼ cup cocoa powder
¼ cup white chocolate chips
Nonstick cooking spray

1. Preheat the oven to 340ºF (171ºC). Spritz a baking pan with nonstick cooking spray.
2. Whisk together the egg, brown sugar, and white sugar in a medium bowl. Mix in the safflower oil and vanilla and stir to combine.
3. Add the flour and cocoa powder and stir just until incorporated. Fold in the white chocolate chips.
4. Scrape the batter into the prepared baking pan.
5. Bake in the preheated oven for 20 minutes, or until the brownie springs back when touched lightly with your fingers.
6. Transfer to a wire rack and let cool for 30 minutes before slicing to serve.

Chocolate Cake with Fresh Blackberries

Prep time: 10 minutes | Cook time: 22 minutes | Serves 8

½ cup butter, at room temperature
2 ounces (57 g) Swerve
4 eggs
1 cup almond flour
1 teaspoon baking soda
$1/_3$ teaspoon baking powder
½ cup cocoa powder
1 teaspoon orange zest
$1/_3$ cup fresh blackberries

1. Preheat the oven to 335ºF (168ºC).
2. With an electric mixer or hand mixer, beat the butter and Swerve until creamy.
3. One at a time, mix in the eggs and beat again until fluffy.
4. Add the almond flour, baking soda, baking powder, cocoa powder, orange zest and mix well. Add the butter mixture to the almond flour mixture and stir until well blended. Fold in the blackberries.
5. Scrape the batter to a baking pan and bake in the preheated oven for 22 minutes. Check the cake for doneness: If a toothpick inserted into the center of the cake comes out clean, it's done.
6. Allow the cake cool on a wire rack to room temperature. Serve immediately.

Chocolate Pineapple Cake

Prep time: 10 minutes | Cook time: 35 to 40 minutes | Serves 4

2 cups flour
4 ounces (113 g) butter, melted
¼ cup sugar
½ pound (227 g) pineapple, chopped
½ cup pineapple

juice
1 ounce (28 g) dark chocolate, grated
1 large egg
2 tablespoons skimmed milk

1. Preheat the oven to 370ºF (188ºC).
2. Grease a cake tin with a little oil or butter.
3. In a bowl, combine the butter and flour to create a crumbly consistency.
4. Add the sugar, chopped pineapple, juice, and grated dark chocolate and mix well.
5. In a separate bowl, combine the egg and milk. Add this mixture to the flour mixture and stir well until a soft dough forms.
6. Pour the mixture into the cake tin and transfer to the oven.
7. Bake for 35 to 40 minutes.
8. Serve immediately.

Ginger Pumpkin Pudding

Prep time: 10 minutes | Cook time: 15 minutes | Serves 4

3 cups pumpkin purée
3 tablespoons honey
1 tablespoon ginger
1 tablespoon

cinnamon
1 teaspoon clove
1 teaspoon nutmeg
1 cup full-fat cream
2 eggs
1 cup sugar

1. Preheat the oven to 390ºF (199ºC).
2. In a bowl, stir all the ingredients together to combine.
3. Scrape the mixture into the a greased dish and transfer to the oven. Bake for 15 minutes. Serve warm.

Candied Cinnamon Apples

Prep time: 15 minutes | Cook time: 12 minutes | Serves 4

1 cup packed light brown sugar
2 teaspoons ground cinnamon

2 medium Granny Smith apples, peeled and diced

1. Preheat the oven to 350ºF (177ºC).
2. Thoroughly combine the brown sugar and cinnamon in a medium bowl.
3. Add the apples to the bowl and stir until well coated. Transfer the apples to a baking pan.
4. Bake in the preheated oven for 9 minutes. Stir the apples once and bake for an additional 3 minutes until softened.
5. Serve warm.

Cinnamon S'mores

Prep time: 5 minutes | Cook time: 10 minutes | Makes 12 s'mores

12 whole cinnamon graham crackers, halved
2 (1.55-ounce / 44-

g) chocolate bars, cut into 12 pieces
12 marshmallows

1. Preheat the oven to 350ºF (177ºC)
2. Working in batches, arrange 6 graham cracker squares in the baking pan in a single layer.
3. Top each square with a piece of chocolate and bake for 2 minutes.
4. Remove the pan and place a marshmallow on each piece of melted chocolate. Bake for another 1 minute.
5. Remove from the pan to a serving plate. Repeat with the remaining 6 graham cracker squares, chocolate pieces, and marshmallows.
6. Serve topped with the remaining graham cracker squares

Carrot, Cherry and Oatmeal Cups

Prep time: 10 minutes | Cook time: 8 minutes | Makes 16 cups

3 tablespoons unsalted butter, at room temperature
¼ cup packed brown sugar
1 tablespoon honey
1 egg white
½ teaspoon vanilla extract
⅓ cup finely grated carrot
½ cup quick-cooking oatmeal
⅓ cup whole-wheat pastry flour
½ teaspoon baking soda
¼ cup dried cherries

1. Preheat the oven to 350°F (177°C)
2. In a medium bowl, beat the butter, brown sugar, and honey until well combined.
3. Add the egg white, vanilla, and carrot. Beat to combine.
4. Stir in the oatmeal, pastry flour, and baking soda.
5. Stir in the dried cherries.
6. Double up 32 mini muffin foil cups to make 16 cups. Fill each with about 4 teaspoons of dough. Bake the cookie cups, 8 at a time, for 8 minutes, or until light golden brown and just set. Serve warm.

Pumpkin Apple Turnovers

Prep time: 10 minutes | Cook time: 10 minutes | Serves 4

1 apple, peeled, quartered, and thinly sliced
½ teaspoon pumpkin pie spice
Juice of ½ lemon
1 tablespoon granulated sugar
Pinch of kosher salt
6 sheets phyllo dough

1. Preheat the oven to 330°F (166°C).
2. In a medium bowl, combine the apple, pumpkin pie spice, lemon juice, granulated sugar, and kosher salt.
3. Cut the phyllo dough sheets into 4 equal pieces and place individual tablespoons of apple filling in the center of each piece, then fold in both sides and roll from front to back.
4. Spray the baking pan with nonstick cooking spray, then place the turnovers in the pan and bake for 10 minutes or until golden brown.
5. Remove the turnovers from the oven and allow to cool on a wire rack for 10 minutes before serving.

Coconut Chocolate Cake

Prep time: 5 minutes | Cook time: 15 minutes | Serves 6

½ cup unsweetened chocolate, chopped
½ stick butter, at room temperature
1 tablespoon liquid stevia
1½ cups coconut flour
2 eggs, whisked
½ teaspoon vanilla extract
A pinch of fine sea salt
Cooking spray

1. Place the chocolate, butter, and stevia in a microwave-safe bowl. Microwave for about 30 seconds until melted.
2. Let the chocolate mixture cool for 5 to 10 minutes.
3. Add the remaining ingredients to the bowl of chocolate mixture and whisk to incorporate.
4. Preheat the oven to 330°F (166°C). Lightly spray a baking pan with cooking spray.
5. Scrape the chocolate mixture into the prepared baking pan.
6. Place the baking pan in the oven and bake for 15 minutes, or until the top springs back lightly when gently pressed with your fingers.
7. Let the cake cool for 5 minutes and serve.

Coconut Chia Pudding

Prep time: 5 minutes | Cook time: 4 minutes | Serves 2

1 cup chia seeds
1 cup unsweetened coconut milk
1 teaspoon liquid stevia

1 tablespoon coconut oil
1 teaspoon butter, melted

1. Preheat the fryer to 360ºF (182ºC).
2. Mix together the chia seeds, coconut milk, and stevia in a large bowl. Add the coconut oil and melted butter and stir until well blended.
3. Divide the mixture evenly between the ramekins, filling only about ²/₃ of the way.
4. Bake in the preheated oven for 4 minutes.
5. Allow to cool for 5 minutes and serve warm.

Vanilla Pound Cake

Prep time: 5 minutes | Cook time: 30 minutes | Serves 8

1 stick butter, at room temperature
1 cup Swerve
4 eggs
1½ cups coconut flour
½ cup buttermilk
½ teaspoon baking soda
½ teaspoon baking

powder
¼ teaspoon salt
1 teaspoon vanilla essence
A pinch of ground star anise
A pinch of freshly grated nutmeg
Cooking spray

1. Preheat the oven to 320ºF (160ºC). Spray a baking pan with cooking spray.
2. With an electric mixer or hand mixer, beat the butter and Swerve until creamy. One at a time, mix in the eggs and whisk until fluffy. Add the remaining ingredients and stir to combine.

3. Transfer the batter to the prepared baking pan. Bake in the preheated oven for 30 minutes until the center of the cake is springy. Rotate the pan halfway through the cooking time.
4. Allow the cake to cool in the pan for 10 minutes before removing and serving.

Peach Blackberry Cobbler with Oats

Prep time: 10 minutes | Cook time: 20 minutes | Serves 4

Filling:
1 (6-ounce / 170-g) package blackberries
1½ cups chopped peaches, cut into ½-inch thick slices
2 teaspoons

arrowroot or cornstarch
2 tablespoons coconut sugar
1 teaspoon lemon juice

Topping:
2 tablespoons sunflower oil
1 tablespoon maple syrup
1 teaspoon vanilla
3 tablespoons coconut sugar

½ cup rolled oats
¹/₃ cup whole-wheat pastry flour
1 teaspoon cinnamon
¼ teaspoon nutmeg
⅛ teaspoon sea salt

Make the Filling:
1. Combine the blackberries, peaches, arrowroot, coconut sugar, and lemon juice in a baking pan.
2. Using a rubber spatula, stir until well incorporated. Set aside.

Make the Topping:
1. Preheat the oven to 320ºF (160ºC)
2. Combine the oil, maple syrup, and vanilla in a mixing bowl and stir well. Whisk in the remaining ingredients. Spread this mixture evenly over the filling.
3. Place the pan in the oven and bake for 20 minutes, or until the topping is crispy and golden brown. Serve warm

Chocolate Pie with Pecans

Prep time: 20 minutes | Cook time: 25 minutes | Serves 8

1 (9-inch) unbaked pie crust
Filling:

2 large eggs	1 cup milk chocolate chips
⅓ cup butter, melted	1½ cups coarsely chopped pecans
1 cup sugar	2 tablespoons bourbon
½ cup all-purpose flour	

1. Preheat the oven to 350ºF (177ºC).
2. Whisk the eggs and melted butter in a large bowl until creamy.
3. Add the sugar and flour and stir to incorporate. Mix in the milk chocolate chips, pecans, and bourbon and stir until well combined.
4. Use a fork to prick holes in the bottom and sides of the pie crust. Pour the prepared filling into the pie crust. Place the pie crust in the baking pan.
5. Bake for 25 minutes until a toothpick inserted in the center comes out clean.
6. Allow the pie cool for 10 minutes in the pan before serving.

Ginger Cinnamon Cookies

Prep time: 15 minutes | Cook time: 12 minutes | Serves 4

4 tablespoons (½ stick) unsalted butter, at room temperature	2 teaspoons ground ginger
2 tablespoons agave nectar	1 teaspoon ground cinnamon
1 large egg	½ teaspoon freshly grated nutmeg
2 tablespoons water	1 teaspoon baking soda
2½ cups almond flour	¼ teaspoon kosher salt
½ cup sugar	

1. Preheat the oven to 325ºF (163ºC).
2. Line the baking pan with parchment paper cut to fit.
3. In a large bowl using a hand mixer, beat together the butter, agave, egg, and water on medium speed until fluffy.
4. Add the almond flour, sugar, ginger, cinnamon, nutmeg, baking soda, and salt. Beat on low speed until well combined.
5. Roll the dough into 2-tablespoon balls and arrange them on the parchment paper. (They don't really spread too much, but try to leave a little room between them.) Bake for 12 minutes, or until the tops of cookies are lightly browned.
6. Transfer to a wire rack and let cool completely.
7. Serve immediately

Mixed Berry Crisp with Coconut Chips

Prep time: 5 minutes | Cook time: 20 minutes | Serves 6

1 tablespoon butter, melted	½ teaspoon ground cinnamon
12 ounces (340 g) mixed berries	¼ teaspoon ground cloves
⅓ cup granulated Swerve	¼ teaspoon grated nutmeg
1 teaspoon pure vanilla extract	½ cup coconut chips, for garnish

1. Preheat the oven to 330ºF (166ºC). Coat a baking pan with melted butter.
2. Put the remaining ingredients except the coconut chips in the prepared baking pan.
3. Bake in the preheated oven for 20 minutes.
4. Serve garnished with the coconut chips.

Apple Cinnamon Fritters

Prep time: 30 minutes | Cook time: 7 to 8 minutes | Serves 6

1 cup chopped, peeled Granny Smith apple
½ cup granulated sugar
1 teaspoon ground cinnamon
1 cup all-purpose flour
1 teaspoon baking powder
1 teaspoon salt
2 tablespoons milk
2 tablespoons butter, melted
1 large egg, beaten
Cooking spray
¼ cup confectioners' sugar (optional)

1. Mix together the apple, granulated sugar, and cinnamon in a small bowl. Allow to sit for 30 minutes.
2. Combine the flour, baking powder, and salt in a medium bowl. Add the milk, butter, and egg and stir to incorporate.
3. Pour the apple mixture into the bowl of flour mixture and stir with a spatula until a dough forms.
4. Make the fritters: On a clean work surface, divide the dough into 12 equal portions and shape into 1-inch balls. Flatten them into patties with your hands.
5. Preheat the oven to 350ºF (177ºC). Line the baking pan with parchment paper and spray it with cooking spray.
6. Transfer the apple fritters onto the parchment paper, evenly spaced but not too close together. Spray the fritters with cooking spray.
7. Bake for 7 to 8 minutes until lightly browned. Flip the fritters halfway through the cooking time.
8. Remove from the pan to a plate and serve with the confectioners' sugar sprinkled on top, if desired.

Blueberry Chocolate Cupcakes

Prep time: 5 minutes | Cook time: 15 minutes | Serves 6

¾ cup granulated erythritol
1¼ cups almond flour
1 teaspoon unsweetened baking powder
3 teaspoons cocoa powder
½ teaspoon baking soda
½ teaspoon ground cinnamon
¼ teaspoon grated nutmeg
⅛ teaspoon salt
½ cup milk
1 stick butter, at room temperature
3 eggs, whisked
1 teaspoon pure rum extract
½ cup blueberries
Cooking spray

1. Preheat the oven to 345ºF (174ºC). Spray a 6-cup muffin tin with cooking spray.
2. In a mixing bowl, combine the erythritol, almond flour, baking powder, cocoa powder, baking soda, cinnamon, nutmeg, and salt and stir until well blended.
3. In another mixing bowl, mix together the milk, butter, egg, and rum extract until thoroughly combined. Slowly and carefully pour this mixture into the bowl of dry mixture. Stir in the blueberries.
4. Spoon the batter into the greased muffin cups, filling each about three-quarters full.
5. Bake for 15 minutes, or until the center is springy and a toothpick inserted in the middle comes out clean.
6. Remove from the oven and place on a wire rack to cool. Serve immediately.

Peppermint Chocolate Cheesecake

Prep time: 5 minutes | Cook time: 18 minutes | Serves 6

Crust:

½ cup butter, melted	2 tablespoons stevia
½ cup coconut flour	Cooking spray

Topping:

4 ounces (113 g) unsweetened baker's chocolate	temperature
	1 teaspoon vanilla extract
1 cup mascarpone cheese, at room	2 drops peppermint extract

1. Preheat the oven to 350ºF (177ºC). Lightly coat a baking pan with cooking spray.
2. In a mixing bowl, whisk together the butter, flour, and stevia until well combined. Transfer the mixture to the prepared baking pan.
3. Place the baking pan in the oven and bake for 18 minutes until a toothpick inserted in the center comes out clean.
4. Remove the crust from the oven to a wire rack to cool.
5. Once cooled completely, place it in the freezer for 20 minutes.
6. When ready, combine all the ingredients for the topping in a small bowl and stir to incorporate.
7. Spread this topping over the crust and let it sit for another 15 minutes in the freezer.
8. Serve chilled.

Coffee Coconut Chocolate Cake

Prep time: 5 minutes | Cook time: 30 minutes | Serves 8

Dry Ingredients:

1½ cups almond flour	1 teaspoon baking powder
½ cup coconut meal	¼ teaspoon salt
⅔ cup Swerve	

Wet Ingredients:

1 egg	½ cup hot strongly brewed coffee
1 stick butter, melted	

Topping:

½ cup confectioner's Swerve	coconut oil
	1 teaspoon ground cinnamon
¼ cup coconut flour	½ teaspoon ground cardamom
3 tablespoons	

1. Preheat the oven to 330ºF (166ºC).
2. In a medium bowl, combine the almond flour, coconut meal, Swerve, baking powder, and salt.
3. In a large bowl, whisk the egg, melted butter, and coffee until smooth.
4. Add the dry mixture to the wet and stir until well incorporated. Transfer the batter to a greased baking pan.
5. Stir together all the ingredients for the topping in a small bowl. Spread the topping over the batter and smooth the top with a spatula.
6. Bake in the preheated oven for 30 minutes, or until the cake springs back when gently pressed with your fingers.
7. Rest for 10 minutes before serving.

Vanilla-Rum Pineapple Galette

Prep time: 10 minutes | Cook time: 40 minutes | Serves 2

¼ medium-size pineapple, peeled, cored, and cut crosswise into ¼-inch-thick slices
2 tablespoons dark rum
1 teaspoon vanilla extract
½ teaspoon kosher salt
Finely grated zest of ½ lime
1 store-bought sheet puff pastry, cut into an 8-inch round
3 tablespoons granulated sugar
2 tablespoons unsalted butter, cubed and chilled
Coconut ice cream, for serving

1. Preheat the oven to 310ºF (154ºC).
2. In a small bowl, combine the pineapple slices, rum, vanilla, salt, and lime zest and let stand for at least 10 minutes to allow the pineapple to soak in the rum.
3. Meanwhile, press the puff pastry round into the bottom and up the sides of a round metal cake pan and use the tines of a fork to dock the bottom and sides.
4. Arrange the pineapple slices on the bottom of the pastry in more or less a single layer, then sprinkle with the sugar and dot with the butter. Drizzle with the leftover juices from the bowl. Put the pan in the oven and bake until the pastry is puffed and golden brown and the pineapple is lightly caramelized on top, about 40 minutes.
5. Transfer the pan to a wire rack to cool for 15 minutes. Unmold the galette from the pan and serve warm with coconut ice cream.

Lemon Poppy Seed Cake

Prep time: 15 minutes | Cook time: 55 minutes | Serves 4

Unsalted butter, at room temperature
1 cup almond flour
½ cup sugar
3 large eggs
¼ cup heavy cream
¼ cup full-fat ricotta cheese
¼ cup coconut oil, melted
2 tablespoons poppy seeds
1 teaspoon baking powder
1 teaspoon pure lemon extract
Grated zest and juice of 1 lemon, plus more zest for garnish

1. Preheat the oven to 325ºF (163ºC).
2. Generously butter a round baking pan. Line the bottom of the pan with parchment paper cut to fit.
3. In a large bowl, combine the almond flour, sugar, eggs, cream, ricotta, coconut oil, poppy seeds, baking powder, lemon extract, lemon zest, and lemon juice. Beat with a hand mixer on medium speed until well blended and fluffy.
4. Pour the batter into the prepared pan. Cover the pan tightly with aluminum foil. Set the pan in the oven and bake for 45 minutes. Remove the foil and bake for 10 to 15 minutes more until a knife (do not use a toothpick) inserted into the center of the cake comes out clean.
5. Let the cake cool in the pan on a wire rack for 10 minutes. Remove the cake from pan and let it cool on the rack for 15 minutes before slicing.
6. Top with additional lemon zest, slice and serve.

Chapter 10 Holiday Specials

Asiago Cheese Bread

Prep time: 37 minutes | Cook time: 24 minutes | Makes 12 balls

2 tablespoons butter, plus more for greasing	flour
	½ teaspoon salt
	1 large egg
½ cup milk	⅔ cup finely grated
1½ cups tapioca	aged Asiago cheese

1. Put the butter in a saucepan and pour in the milk, heat over medium heat until the liquid boils. Keep stirring.
2. Turn off the heat and mix in the tapioca flour and salt to form a soft dough. Transfer the dough in a large bowl, then wrap the bowl in plastic and let sit for 15 minutes.
3. Break the egg in the bowl of dough and whisk with a hand mixer for 2 minutes or until a sanity dough forms. Fold the cheese in the dough. Cover the bowl in plastic again and let sit for 10 more minutes.
4. Preheat the oven to 375ºF (191ºC). Grease a cake pan with butter.
5. Scoop 2 tablespoons of the dough into the cake pan. Repeat with the remaining dough to make dough 12 balls. Keep a little distance between each two balls. You may need to work in batches to avoid overcrowding.
6. Place the cake pan in the preheated oven.
7. Bake for 12 minutes or until the balls are golden brown and fluffy. Flip the balls halfway through the cooking time.
8. Remove the balls from the oven and allow to cool for 5 minutes before serving.

Monkey Bread with Peacans

Prep time: 15 minutes | Cook time: 25 minutes | Serves 6 to 8

1 (16.3-ounce / 462-g) can store-bought refrigerated biscuit dough	allspice
	⅛ teaspoon ground cloves
¼ cup packed light brown sugar	4 tablespoons (½ stick) unsalted butter, melted
1 teaspoon ground cinnamon	½ cup powdered sugar
½ teaspoon freshly grated nutmeg	2 teaspoons bourbon
½ teaspoon ground ginger	2 tablespoons chopped candied cherries
½ teaspoon kosher salt	2 tablespoons chopped pecans
¼ teaspoon ground	

1. Preheat the oven to 310ºF (154ºC).
2. Open the can and separate the biscuits, then cut each into quarters. Toss the biscuit quarters in a large bowl with the brown sugar, cinnamon, nutmeg, ginger, salt, allspice, and cloves until evenly coated. Transfer the dough pieces and any sugar left in the bowl to a round cake pan, metal cake pan, or foil pan and drizzle evenly with the melted butter. Put the pan in the oven and bake until the monkey bread is golden brown and cooked through in the middle, about 25 minutes. Transfer the pan to a wire rack and let cool completely. Unmold from the pan.
3. In a small bowl, whisk the powdered sugar and the bourbon into a smooth glaze. Drizzle the glaze over the cooled monkey bread and, while the glaze is still wet, sprinkle with the cherries and pecans to serve.

Maple Vanilla Pecan Tart

Prep time: 2hours 25 minutes | Cook time: 30 minutes | Serves 8

Tart Crust:

¼ cup firmly packed brown sugar	1 cup all-purpose flour
$^1/_3$ cup butter, softened	¼ teaspoon kosher salt

Filling:

¼ cup whole milk	syrup
4 tablespoons butter, diced	1½ cups finely chopped pecans
½ cup packed brown sugar	¼ teaspoon pure vanilla extract
¼ cup pure maple	¼ teaspoon sea salt

1. Preheat the oven to 350ºF (177ºC). Line a baking pan with aluminum foil, then spritz the pan with cooking spray.
2. Stir the brown sugar and butter in a bowl with a hand mixer until puffed, then add the flour and salt and stir until crumbled.
3. Pour the mixture in the prepared baking pan and tilt the pan to coat the bottom evenly.
4. Arrange the pan in the preheated oven. Bake for 13 minutes or until the crust is golden brown.
5. Meanwhile, pour the milk, butter, sugar, and maple syrup in a saucepan. Stir to mix well. Bring to a simmer, then cook for 1 more minute. Stir constantly.
6. Turn off the heat and mix the pecans and vanilla into the filling mixture.
7. Pour the filling mixture over the golden crust and spread with a spatula to coat the crust evenly.
8. Bake in the oven for an additional 12 minutes or until the filling mixture is set and frothy.
9. Remove the baking pan from the oven and sprinkle with salt. Allow to sit for 10 minutes or until cooled.
10. Transfer the pan to the refrigerator to chill for at least 2 hours, then remove the aluminum foil and slice to serve.

Vanilla Butter Cake

Prep time: 25 minutes | Cook time: 20 minutes | Serves 8

1 cup all-purpose flour	butter, at room temperature
1¼ teaspoons baking powder	2 large eggs
¼ teaspoon salt	1 large egg yolk
½ cup plus 1½ tablespoons granulated white sugar	2½ tablespoons milk
9½ tablespoons	1 teaspoon vanilla extract
	Cooking spray

1. Preheat the oven to 325ºF (163ºC). Spritz a cake pan with cooking spray.
2. Combine the flour, baking powder, and salt in a large bowl. Stir to mix well.
3. Whip the sugar and butter in a separate bowl with a hand mixer on medium speed for 3 minutes.
4. Whip the eggs, egg yolk, milk, and vanilla extract into the sugar and butter mix with a hand mixer.
5. Pour in the flour mixture and whip with hand mixer until sanity and smooth.
6. Scrape the batter into the cake pan and level the batter with a spatula.
7. Place the cake pan in the preheated oven.
8. Bake for 20 minutes or until a toothpick inserted in the center comes out clean. Check the doneness during the last 5 minutes of the baking.
9. Invert the cake on a cooling rack and allow to cool for 15 minutes before slicing to serve.

Eggnog Bread with Pecans and Fruit

Prep time: 10 minutes | Cook time: 18 minutes | Serves 6 to 8

1 cup flour, plus more for dusting
¼ cup sugar
1 teaspoon baking powder
¼ teaspoon salt
¼ teaspoon nutmeg
½ cup eggnog
1 egg yolk
1 tablespoon plus

1 teaspoon butter, melted
¼ cup pecans
¼ cup chopped candied fruit (cherries, pineapple, or mixed fruits)
Cooking spray

1. Preheat the oven to 360°F (182°C).
2. In a medium bowl, stir together the flour, sugar, baking powder, salt, and nutmeg.
3. Add eggnog, egg yolk, and butter. Mix well but do not beat.
4. Stir in nuts and fruit.
5. Spray a baking pan with cooking spray and dust with flour.
6. Spread batter into prepared pan and bake for 18 minutes or until top is dark golden brown and bread starts to pull away from sides of pan.
7. Serve immediately.

Breaded Olives with Thyme

Prep time: 10 minutes | Cook time: 6 minutes | Serves 4

12 ounces (340 g) pitted black extra-large olives
¼ cup all-purpose flour
1 cup panko bread crumbs
2 teaspoons dried thyme

1 teaspoon red pepper flakes
1 teaspoon smoked paprika
1 egg beaten with 1 tablespoon water
Vegetable oil for spraying

1. Preheat the oven to 425°F (218°C).

2. Drain the olives and place them on a paper towel-lined plate to dry.
3. Put the flour on a plate. Combine the panko, thyme, red pepper flakes, and paprika on a separate plate. Dip an olive in the flour, shaking off any excess, then coat with egg mixture. Dredge the olive in the panko mixture, pressing to make the crumbs adhere, and place the breaded olive on a platter. Repeat with the remaining olives.
4. Spray the olives with oil and place them in a single layer in the baking pan. Bake for 6 minutes until the breading is browned and crispy. Serve warm

Pigs in a Blanket with Sesame Seeds

Prep time: 10 minutes | Cook time: 8 minutes per batch | Makes 16 rolls

1 can refrigerated crescent roll dough
1 small package mini smoked sausages, patted dry

2 tablespoons melted butter
2 teaspoons sesame seeds
1 teaspoon onion powder

1. Preheat the oven to 330°F (166°C).
2. Place the crescent roll dough on a clean work surface and separate into 8 pieces. Cut each piece in half and you will have 16 triangles.
3. Make the pigs in the blanket: Arrange each sausage on each dough triangle, then roll the sausages up.
4. Brush the pigs with melted butter and place half of the pigs in the blanket in the preheated oven. Sprinkle with sesame seeds and onion powder.
5. Bake for 8 minutes or until the pigs are fluffy and golden brown. Flip the pigs halfway through.
6. Serve immediately.

Risotto Croquettes with Tomato Sauce

Prep time: 1 hour 40 minutes | Cook time: 1 hour | Serves 6

Risotto Croquettes:

4 tablespoons unsalted butter	2 ounces (57 g) fresh Mozzarella cheese
1 small yellow onion, minced	¼ cup peas
1 cup Arborio rice	2 tablespoons water
3½ cups chicken stock	½ cup all-purpose flour
½ cup dry white wine	1½ cups panko bread crumbs
3 eggs	Kosher salt and ground black pepper, to taste
Zest of 1 lemon	
½ cup grated Parmesan cheese	Cooking spray

Tomato Sauce:

2 tablespoons extra-virgin olive oil	g) can crushed tomatoes
4 cloves garlic, minced	2 teaspoons granulated sugar
¼ teaspoon red pepper flakes	Kosher salt and ground black pepper, to taste
1 (28-ounce / 794-	

1. Melt the butter in a pot over medium heat, then add the onion and salt to taste. Sauté for 5 minutes or until the onion in translucent.
2. Add the rice and stir to coat well. Cook for 3 minutes or until the rice is lightly browned. Pour in the chicken stock and wine.
3. Bring to a boil. Then cook for 20 minutes or until the rice is tender and liquid is almost absorbed.
4. Make the risotto: When the rice is cooked, break the egg into the pot. Add the lemon zest and Parmesan cheese. Sprinkle with salt and ground black pepper. Stir to mix well.
5. Pour the risotto in a baking sheet, then level with a spatula to spread the risotto evenly. Wrap the baking sheet in plastic and refrigerate for 1 hour.
6. Meanwhile, heat the olive oil in a saucepan over medium heat until shimmering.
7. Add the garlic and sprinkle with red pepper flakes. Sauté for a minute or until fragrant.
8. Add the crushed tomatoes and sprinkle with sugar. Stir to mix well. Bring to a boil. Reduce the heat to low and simmer for 15 minutes or until lightly thickened. Sprinkle with salt and pepper to taste. Set aside until ready to serve.
9. Remove the risotto from the refrigerator. Scoop the risotto into twelve 2-inch balls, then flatten the balls with your hands.
10. Arrange a about ½-inch piece of Mozzarella and 5 peas in the center of each flattened ball, then wrap them back into balls.
11. Transfer the balls in a baking sheet lined with parchment paper, then refrigerate for 15 minutes or until firm.
12. Preheat the oven to 400ºF (204ºC).
13. Whisk the remaining 2 eggs with 2 tablespoons of water in a bowl. Pour the flour in a second bowl and pour the panko in a third bowl.
14. Dredge the risotto balls in the bowl of flour first, then into the eggs, and then into the panko. Shake the excess off.
15. Transfer the balls in the preheated oven and spritz with cooking spray. You may need to work in batches to avoid overcrowding.
16. Bake for 10 minutes or until golden brown. Flip the balls halfway through.
17. Serve the risotto balls with the tomato sauce.

Chapter 11 Fast and Easy Everyday Favorites

Buttery Egg and Broccoli Bake

Prep time: 5 minutes | Cook time: 6 minutes | Serves 1

4 egg yolks
¼ cup butter, melted
2 cups coconut flour

Salt and pepper, to taste
2 cups broccoli florets

1. Preheat the oven to 425ºF (218ºC).
2. In a bowl, whisk the egg yolks and melted butter together. Throw in the coconut flour, salt and pepper, then stir again to combine well.
3. Dip each broccoli floret into the mixture and place in the baking pan. Bake for 8 minutes in batches if necessary. Take care when removing them from the oven and serve immediately.

Baked Chicken Wings

Prep time: 5 minutes | Cook time: 41 minutes | Serves 6

2 pounds (907 g) chicken wings, tips

removed
⅛ teaspoon salt

1. Preheat the oven to 425ºF (218ºC). Season the wings with salt.
2. Working in 2 batches, place half the chicken wings in the baking pan and bake for 18 minutes, or until the skin is browned and cooked through, turning the wings with tongs halfway through cooking.
3. Combine both batches in the oven and bake for 5 minutes more. Transfer to a large bowl and serve immediately.

Cheddar Sausage Balls

Prep time: 5 minutes | Cook time: 18 minutes | Serves 6

12 ounces (340 g) Jimmy Dean's Sausage
6 ounces (170 g)

shredded Cheddar cheese
10 Cheddar cubes

1. Preheat the oven to 400ºF (204ºC).
2. Mix the shredded cheese and sausage.
3. Divide the mixture into 12 equal parts to be stuffed.
4. Add a cube of cheese to the center of the sausage and roll into balls.
5. Bake for 18 minutes, or until crisp.
6. Serve immediately.

Carrot Chips with Parsley

Prep time: 5 minutes | Cook time: 15 minutes | Makes 3 cups

3 large carrots, peeled and sliced into long and thick chips diagonally
1 tablespoon granulated garlic
1 teaspoon salt

¼ teaspoon ground black pepper
1 tablespoon olive oil
1 tablespoon finely chopped fresh parsley

1. Preheat the oven to 360ºF (182ºC).
2. Toss the carrots with garlic, salt, ground black pepper, and olive oil in a large bowl to coat well.
3. Place the carrots in the preheated oven. Bake for 15 minutes or until the carrot chips are soft. Stir halfway through.
4. Serve the carrot chips with parsley on top.

Beef Hot Dog with Bacon

Prep time: 5 minutes | Cook time: 10 minutes | Serves 4

4 slices sugar-free bacon
4 beef hot dogs

1. Preheat the oven to 370ºF (188ºC).
2. Take a slice of bacon and wrap it around the hot dog, securing it with a toothpick. Repeat with the other pieces of bacon and hot dogs, placing each wrapped dog in the baking pan.
3. Bake for 10 minutes, turning halfway through.
4. Once hot and crispy, the hot dogs are ready to serve.

Manchego Frico with Cumin Seeds

Prep time: 5 minutes | Cook time: 6 minutes | Serves 2

1 cup shredded aged Manchego cheese	½ teaspoon cumin seeds
1 teaspoon all-purpose flour	¼ teaspoon cracked black pepper

1. Preheat the oven to 400ºF (204ºC). Line the baking pan with parchment paper.
2. Combine the cheese and flour in a bowl. Stir to mix well. Spread the mixture in the pan into a 4-inch round.
3. Combine the cumin and black pepper in a small bowl. Stir to mix well. Sprinkle the cumin mixture over the cheese round.
4. Bake for 6 minutes or until the cheese is lightly browned and frothy.
5. Use tongs to transfer the cheese wafer onto a plate and slice to serve.

Green Beans Bake with Lemon Pepper

Prep time: 5 minutes | Cook time: 10 minutes | Makes 2 cups

½ teaspoon lemon pepper	1 tablespoon olive oil
2 teaspoons granulated garlic	2 cups fresh green beans, trimmed and snapped in half
½ teaspoon salt	

1. Preheat the oven to 370ºF (188ºC).
2. Combine the lemon pepper, garlic, salt, and olive oil in a bowl. Stir to mix well.
3. Add the green beans to the bowl of mixture and toss to coat well.
4. Arrange the green beans in the preheated oven. Bake for 10 minutes or until tender and crispy.
5. Serve immediately.

Green Beans and Bacon Bake

Prep time: 15 minutes | Cook time: 12 minutes | Serves 4

2 (14.5-ounce / 411-g) cans cut green beans, drained	vinegar
	1 teaspoon freshly squeezed lemon juice
4 bacon slices, air-fried and diced	½ teaspoon salt
¼ cup minced onion	½ teaspoon freshly ground black pepper
1 tablespoon distilled white	Cooking spray

1. Preheat the oven to 400ºF (204ºC).
2. Spritz a baking pan with oil. In the prepared pan, stir together the green beans, bacon, onion, vinegar, lemon juice, salt, and pepper until blended.
3. Bake for 5 minutes. Stir the green beans and bake for 7 minutes more until soft.
4. Serve immediately.

Old Bay Shrimp with Cayenne

Prep time: 7 minutes | Cook time: 12 minutes | Makes 2 cups

½ teaspoon Old Bay Seasoning
1 teaspoon ground cayenne pepper
½ teaspoon paprika
1 tablespoon olive oil

⅛ teaspoon salt
½ pound (227 g) shrimps, peeled and deveined
Juice of half a lemon

1. Preheat the oven to 425ºF (218ºC).
2. Combine the Old Bay Seasoning, cayenne pepper, paprika, olive oil, and salt in a large bowl, then add the shrimps and toss to coat well.
3. Put the shrimps in the baking pan. Bake for 12 minutes or until opaque. Flip the shrimps halfway through.
4. Serve the shrimps with lemon juice on top.

Okra Chips

Prep time: 5 minutes | Cook time: 16 minutes | Serves 6

2 pounds (907 g) fresh okra pods, cut into 1-inch pieces
2 tablespoons

canola oil
1 teaspoon coarse sea salt

1. Preheat the oven to 425ºF (218ºC).
2. Stir the oil and salt in a bowl to mix well. Add the okra and toss to coat well.
3. Place the okra in the baking pan. Bake for 18 minutes or until lightly browned. Stir at least three times during the cooking time.
4. Serve immediately.

Baked Peanuts with Hot Pepper Sauce

Prep time: 5 minutes | Cook time: 6 minutes | Serves 9

3 cups shelled raw peanuts
1 tablespoon hot red pepper sauce

3 tablespoons granulated white sugar

1. Preheat the oven to 425ºF (218ºC).
2. Put the peanuts in a large bowl, then drizzle with hot red pepper sauce and sprinkle with sugar. Toss to coat well.
3. Pour the peanuts in the baking pan. Bake for 6 minutes or until the peanuts are crispy and browned.
4. Serve immediately.

Chile Toast with Mozzarella Cheese

Prep time: 5 minutes | Cook time: 5 minutes | Serves 1

2 tablespoons grated Parmesan cheese
2 tablespoons grated Mozzarella cheese
2 teaspoons salted butter, at room

temperature
10 to 15 thin slices serrano chile or jalapeño
2 slices sourdough bread
½ teaspoon black pepper

1. Preheat the oven to 325ºF (163ºC).
2. In a small bowl, stir together the Parmesan, Mozzarella, butter, and chiles.
3. Spread half the mixture onto one side of each slice of bread. Sprinkle with the pepper. Place the slices, cheese-side up, in the baking pan. Bake for 5 minutes, or until the cheese has melted and started to brown slightly.
4. Serve immediately.

Cheese Capicola Sandwich with Mayo

Prep time: 5 minutes | Cook time: 8 minutes | Serves 2

2 tablespoons mayonnaise
4 thick slices sourdough bread

4 thick slices Brie cheese
8 slices hot capicola

1. Preheat the oven to 350ºF (177ºC).
2. Spread the mayonnaise on one side of each slice of bread. Place 2 slices of bread in the baking pan, mayonnaise-side down.
3. Place the slices of Brie and capicola on the bread and cover with the remaining two slices of bread, mayonnaise-side up.
4. Bake for 8 minutes, or until the cheese has melted.
5. Serve immediately.

Halloumi Cheese Bake with Greek Salsa

Prep time: 15 minutes | Cook time: 6 minutes | Serves 4

Salsa:
1 small shallot, finely diced
3 garlic cloves, minced
2 tablespoons fresh lemon juice
2 tablespoons extra-virgin olive oil
1 teaspoon freshly cracked black pepper
Pinch of kosher salt

½ cup finely diced English cucumber
1 plum tomato, deseeded and finely diced
2 teaspoons chopped fresh parsley
1 teaspoon snipped fresh dill
1 teaspoon snipped fresh oregano

Cheese:
8 ounces (227 g) Halloumi cheese, sliced into ½-inch-thick pieces
1 tablespoon extra-virgin olive oil

1. Preheat the oven to 375ºF (191ºC).
2. For the salsa: Combine the shallot, garlic, lemon juice, olive oil, pepper, and salt in a medium bowl. Add the cucumber, tomato, parsley, dill, and oregano. Toss gently to combine; set aside.
3. For the cheese: Place the cheese slices in a medium bowl. Drizzle with the olive oil. Toss gently to coat. Arrange the cheese in a single layer in the baking pan. Bake for 6 minutes.
4. Divide the cheese among four serving plates. Top with the salsa and serve immediately.

Cheddar Jalapeño Poppers with Bacon

Prep time: 5 minutes | Cook time: 12 minutes | Serves 6

6 large jalapeños
4 ounces (113 g) ⅓-less-fat cream cheese
¼ cup shredded reduced-fat sharp

Cheddar cheese
2 scallions, green tops only, sliced
6 slices center-cut bacon, halved

1. Preheat the oven to 325ºF (163ºC).
2. Wearing rubber gloves, halve the jalapeños lengthwise to make 12 pieces. Scoop out the seeds and membranes and discard.
3. In a medium bowl, combine the cream cheese, Cheddar, and scallions. Using a small spoon or spatula, fill the jalapeños with the cream cheese filling. Wrap a bacon strip around each pepper and secure with a toothpick.
4. Working in batches, place the stuffed peppers in a single layer in the baking pan. Bake for about 12 minutes, until the peppers are tender, the bacon is browned and crisp, and the cheese is melted.
5. Serve warm.

Potato Patties with Colby Cheese

Prep time: 5 minutes | Cook time: 10 minutes | Serves 8

2 pounds (907 g) white potatoes
½ cup finely chopped scallions
½ teaspoon freshly ground black pepper, or more to taste
1 tablespoon fine

sea salt
½ teaspoon hot paprika
2 cups shredded Colby cheese
¼ cup canola oil
1 cup crushed crackers

1. Preheat the oven to 360ºF (182ºC).
2. Boil the potatoes until soft. Dry them off and peel them before mashing thoroughly, leaving no lumps.
3. Combine the mashed potatoes with scallions, pepper, salt, paprika, and cheese.
4. Mold the mixture into balls with your hands and press with your palm to flatten them into patties.
5. In a shallow dish, combine the canola oil and crushed crackers. Coat the patties in the crumb mixture.
6. Bake the patties for about 10 minutes, in multiple batches if necessary.
7. Serve hot.

Cherry Tomato Bake with Basil

Prep time: 5 minutes | Cook time: 4 to 6 minutes | Serves 2

2 cups cherry tomatoes
1 clove garlic, thinly sliced
1 teaspoon olive oil
⅛ teaspoon kosher

salt
1 tablespoon freshly chopped basil, for topping
Cooking spray

1. Preheat the oven to 360ºF (182ºC). Spritz the oven baking pan with cooking spray and set aside.

2. In a large bowl, toss together the cherry tomatoes, sliced garlic, olive oil, and kosher salt. Spread the mixture in an even layer in the prepared pan.
3. Bake in the preheated oven for 4 to 6 minutes, or until the tomatoes become soft and wilted.
4. Transfer to a bowl and rest for 5 minutes. Top with the chopped basil and serve warm.

Panko-Chorizo Scotch Eggs

Prep time: 5 minutes | Cook time: 15 to 20 minutes | Makes 4 eggs

1 pound (454 g) Mexican chorizo or other seasoned sausage meat
4 soft-boiled eggs plus 1 raw egg

1 tablespoon water
½ cup all-purpose flour
1 cup panko bread crumbs
Cooking spray

1. Divide the chorizo into 4 equal portions. Flatten each portion into a disc. Place a soft-boiled egg in the center of each disc. Wrap the chorizo around the egg, encasing it completely. Place the encased eggs on a plate and chill for at least 30 minutes.
2. Preheat the oven to 360ºF (182ºC).
3. Beat the raw egg with 1 tablespoon of water. Place the flour on a small plate and the panko on a second plate. Working with 1 egg at a time, roll the encased egg in the flour, then dip it in the egg mixture. Dredge the egg in the panko and place on a plate. Repeat with the remaining eggs.
4. Spray the eggs with oil and place in the baking pan. Bake for 10 minutes. Turn and bake for an additional 5 to 10 minutes, or until browned and crisp on all sides.
5. Serve immediately.

Chicken Wings with Hot Sauce

Prep time: 5 minutes | Cook time: 30 minutes | Makes 16 wings

16 chicken wings
3 tablespoons hot sauce

Cooking spray

1. Preheat the oven to 360ºF (182ºC). Spritz the baking pan with cooking spray.
2. Arrange the chicken wings in the pan. You need to work in batches to avoid overcrowding.
3. Bake for 15 minutes or until well browned. Flip the chicken wings at lease three times during the cooking.
4. Transfer the wings on a plate and serve with hot sauce.

Shrimp, Sausage and Potato Bake

Prep time: 10 minutes | Cook time: 18 minutes | Serves 2

1 ear corn, husk and silk removed, cut into 2-inch rounds
8 ounces (227 g) red potatoes, unpeeled, cut into 1-inch pieces
2 teaspoons Old Bay Seasoning, divided
2 teaspoons vegetable oil, divided
¼ teaspoon ground black pepper

8 ounces (227 g) large shrimps (about 12 shrimps), deveined
6 ounces (170 g) andouille or chorizo sausage, cut into 1-inch pieces
2 garlic cloves, minced
1 tablespoon chopped fresh parsley

1. Preheat the oven to 400ºF (204ºC).
2. Put the corn rounds and potatoes in a large bowl. Sprinkle with 1 teaspoon of Old Bay seasoning and drizzle with vegetable oil. Toss to coat well.
3. Transfer the corn rounds and potatoes on a baking sheet, then put in the preheated oven.
4. Bake for 12 minutes or until soft and browned.
5. Meanwhile, cut slits into the shrimps but be careful not to cut them through. Combine the shrimps, sausage, remaining Old Bay seasoning, and remaining vegetable oil in the large bowl. Toss to coat well.
6. When the baking of the potatoes and corn rounds is complete, add the shrimps and sausage and bake for 6 more minutes or until the shrimps are opaque.
7. When the baking is finished, serve them on a plate and spread with parsley before serving.

Chapter 12 Casseroles, Frittatas, and Quiches

Feta-Cheddar Vegetable Frittata

Prep time: 15 minutes | Cook time: 21 minutes | Serves 2

4 eggs
¼ cup milk
Sea salt and ground black pepper, to taste
1 zucchini, sliced
½ bunch asparagus, sliced
½ cup mushrooms, sliced
½ cup spinach, shredded
½ cup red onion, sliced
½ tablespoon olive oil
5 tablespoons feta cheese, crumbled
4 tablespoons Cheddar cheese, grated
¼ bunch chives, minced

1. In a bowl, mix the eggs, milk, salt and pepper.
2. Over a medium heat, sauté the vegetables for 6 minutes with the olive oil in a nonstick pan.
3. Put some parchment paper in the base of a baking tin. Pour in the vegetables, followed by the egg mixture. Top with the feta and grated Cheddar.
4. Preheat the oven to 320ºF (160ºC).
5. Transfer the baking tin to the oven and bake for 15 minutes. Remove the frittata from the oven and leave to cool for 5 minutes.
6. Top with the minced chives and serve.

Asparagus and Grits Casserole

Prep time: 5 minutes | Cook time: 31 minutes | Serves 4

10 fresh asparagus spears, cut into 1-inch pieces
2 cups cooked grits, cooled to room temperature
2 teaspoons Worcestershire sauce
1 egg, beaten
½ teaspoon garlic powder
¼ teaspoon salt
2 slices provolone cheese, crushed
Cooking spray

1. Preheat the oven to 425ºF (218ºC). Spritz a baking pan with cooking spray.
2. Set the asparagus in the pan. Spritz the asparagus with cooking spray. Bake for 6 minutes or until lightly browned and crispy.
3. Meanwhile, combine the grits, Worcestershire sauce, egg, garlic powder, and salt in a bowl. Stir to mix well.
4. Pour half of the grits mixture in the pan, then spread with fried asparagus.
5. Spoon half of grits mixture into oven baking pan and top with asparagus. Spread the cheese over the asparagus and pour the remaining grits over.
6. Place the baking pan in the preheated oven. Bake for 25 minutes or until the egg is set and lightly browned.
7. Serve immediately.

Corn Casserole with Bell Pepper

Prep time: 10 minutes | Cook time: 20 minutes | Serves 4

1 cup corn kernels	2 tablespoons
¼ cup bell pepper, finely chopped	melted unsalted butter
½ cup low-fat milk	1 tablespoon
1 large egg, beaten	granulated sugar
½ cup yellow cornmeal	Pinch of cayenne pepper
½ cup all-purpose flour	¼ teaspoon kosher salt
½ teaspoon baking powder	Cooking spray

1. Preheat the oven to 330ºF (166ºC). Spritz a baking pan with cooking spray.
2. Combine all the ingredients in a large bowl. Stir to mix well. Pour the mixture into the baking pan.
3. Place the pan in the preheated oven. Bake for 20 minutes or until lightly browned and set.
4. Remove the baking pan from the oven and serve immediately.

Tomato, Carrot and Broccoli Quiche

Prep time: 6 minutes | Cook time: 14 minutes | Serves 4

4 eggs	¼ cup crumbled feta cheese
1 teaspoon dried thyme	1 cup grated Cheddar cheese
1 cup whole milk	1 teaspoon chopped parsley
1 steamed carrots, diced	Salt and ground black pepper, to taste
2 cups steamed broccoli florets	Cooking spray
2 medium tomatoes, diced	

1. Preheat the oven to 350ºF (177ºC). Spritz a baking pan with cooking spray.
2. Whisk together the eggs, thyme, salt, and ground black pepper in a bowl and fold in the milk while mixing.
3. Put the carrots, broccoli, and tomatoes in the prepared baking pan, then spread with feta cheese and ½ cup Cheddar cheese. Pour the egg mixture over, then scatter with remaining Cheddar on top.
4. Put the pan in the preheated oven. Bake for 14 minutes or until the eggs are set and the quiche is puffed.
5. Remove the quiche from the oven and top with chopped parsley, then slice to serve.

Prosciutto Casserole with Pepper Jack

Prep time: 5 minutes | Cook time: 10 minutes | Serves 2

1 cup day-old whole grain bread, cubed	chopped
3 large eggs, beaten	1 ounce (28 g) Pepper Jack cheese, roughly chopped
2 tablespoons water	1 tablespoon chopped fresh chives
⅛ teaspoon kosher salt	Nonstick cooking spray
1 ounce (28 g) prosciutto, roughly	

1. Preheat the oven to 360ºF (182ºC).
2. Spray a baking pan with nonstick cooking spray, then place the bread cubes in the pan. Transfer the baking pan to the oven.
3. In a medium bowl, stir together the beaten eggs and water, then stir in the kosher salt, prosciutto, cheese, and chives.
4. Pour the egg mixture over the bread cubes and bake for 10 minutes, or until the eggs are set and the top is golden brown.
5. Serve warm.

Feta Chorizo and Potato Frittata

Prep time: 8 minutes | Cook time: 12 minutes | Serves 4

2 tablespoons olive oil
1 chorizo, sliced
4 eggs
½ cup corn
1 large potato, boiled and cubed
1 tablespoon chopped parsley
½ cup feta cheese, crumbled
Salt and ground black pepper, to taste

1. Preheat the oven to 330ºF (166ºC).
2. Heat the olive oil in a nonstick skillet over medium heat until shimmering.
3. Add the chorizo and cook for 4 minutes or until golden brown.
4. Whisk the eggs in a bowl, then sprinkle with salt and ground black pepper.
5. Mix the remaining ingredients in the egg mixture, then pour the chorizo and its fat into a baking pan. Pour in the egg mixture.
6. Place the pan in the preheated oven. Bake for 8 minutes or until the eggs are set.
7. Serve immediately.

Mushroom and Beef Casserole

Prep time: 10 minutes | Cook time: 25 minutes | Serves 4

1½ pounds (680 g) beef steak
1 ounce (28 g) dry onion soup mix
2 cups sliced mushrooms
1 (14.5-ounce / 411-g) can cream
of mushroom soup
½ cup beef broth
¼ cup red wine
3 garlic cloves, minced
1 whole onion, chopped

1. Preheat the oven to 360ºF (182ºC).
2. Put the beef steak in a large bowl, then sprinkle with dry onion soup mix. Toss to coat well.
3. Combine the mushrooms with mushroom soup, beef broth, red wine, garlic, and onion in a large bowl. Stir to mix well.
4. Transfer the beef steak in a baking pan, then pour in the mushroom mixture.
5. Place the pan in the preheated oven. Bake for 25 minutes or until the mushrooms are soft and the beef is well browned.
6. Remove the baking pan from the oven and serve immediately.

Broccoli and Chicken Sausage Casserole

Prep time: 10 minutes | Cook time: 20 minutes | Serves 8

10 eggs
1 cup Cheddar cheese, shredded and divided
¾ cup heavy whipping cream
1 (12-ounce / 340-g) package cooked chicken sausage
1 cup broccoli, chopped
2 cloves garlic, minced
½ tablespoon salt
¼ tablespoon ground black pepper
Cooking spray

1. Preheat the oven to 400ºF (204ºC). Spritz a baking pan with cooking spray.
2. Whisk the eggs with Cheddar and cream in a large bowl to mix well.
3. Combine the cooked sausage, broccoli, garlic, salt, and ground black pepper in a separate bowl. Stir to mix well.
4. Pour the sausage mixture into the baking pan, then spread the egg mixture over to cover.
5. Place the baking pan in the preheated oven. Bake for 20 minutes or until the eggs are set and a toothpick inserted in the center comes out clean.
6. Serve immediately.

Cheddar Scallion and Parsley Frittata

Prep time: 10 minutes | Cook time: 20 minutes | Serves 4

½ cup shredded Cheddar cheese
½ cup half-and-half
4 large eggs
2 tablespoons chopped scallion greens
2 tablespoons

chopped fresh parsley
½ teaspoon kosher salt
½ teaspoon ground black pepper
Cooking spray

1. Preheat the oven to 300ºF (149ºC). Spritz a baking pan with cooking spray.
2. Whisk together all the ingredients in a large bowl, then pour the mixture into the prepared baking pan.
3. Set the pan in the preheated oven and bake for 20 minutes or until set.
4. Serve immediately.

Cheddar Broccoli Casserole

Prep time: 5 minutes | Cook time: 30 minutes | Serves 6

4 cups broccoli florets
¼ cup heavy whipping cream
½ cup sharp Cheddar cheese,

shredded
¼ cup ranch dressing
Kosher salt and ground black pepper, to taste

1. Preheat the oven to 375ºF (191ºC).
2. Combine all the ingredients in a large bowl. Toss to coat well broccoli well.
3. Pour the mixture into a baking pan, then transfer the pan in the preheated oven. Bake for 30 minutes or until the broccoli is tender.
4. Remove the baking pan from the oven and serve immediately.

Pumpkin-Cauliflower Casserole with Pecans

Prep time: 15 minutes | Cook time: 50 minutes | Serves 6

1 cup chicken broth
2 cups cauliflower florets
1 cup canned pumpkin purée
¼ cup heavy cream
1 teaspoon vanilla extract
2 large eggs, beaten

$^1/_3$ cup unsalted butter, melted, plus more for greasing the pan
¼ cup sugar
1 teaspoon fine sea salt
Chopped fresh parsley leaves, for garnish

Topping:
½ cup blanched almond flour
1 cup chopped pecans

$^1/_3$ cup unsalted butter, melted
½ cup sugar

1. Preheat the oven to 350ºF (177ºC).
2. Pour the chicken broth in a baking pan, then add the cauliflower.
3. Place the baking pan in the oven. Bake for 20 minutes or until soft.
4. Meanwhile, combine the ingredients for the topping in a large bowl. Stir to mix well.
5. Pat the cauliflower dry with paper towels, then place in a food processor and pulse with pumpkin purée, heavy cream, vanilla extract, eggs, butter, sugar, and salt until smooth.
6. Clean the baking pan and grease with more butter, then pour the purée mixture in the pan. Spread the topping over the mixture.
7. Place the baking pan in the preheated oven. Bake for 30 minutes or until the topping is lightly browned.
8. Remove the casserole from the oven and serve with fresh parsley on top.

Pork Gratin with Ricotta Cheese

Prep time: 15 minutes | Cook time: 21 minutes | Serves 4

2 tablespoons olive oil
2 pounds (907 g) pork tenderloin, cut into serving-size pieces
1 teaspoon dried marjoram
¼ teaspoon chili powder
1 teaspoon coarse sea salt

½ teaspoon freshly ground black pepper
1 cup Ricotta cheese
1½ cups chicken broth
1 tablespoon mustard
Cooking spray

1. Preheat the oven to 350ºF (177ºC). Spritz a baking pan with cooking spray.
2. Heat the olive oil in a nonstick skillet over medium-high heat until shimmering.
3. Add the pork and sauté for 6 minutes or until lightly browned.
4. Transfer the pork to the prepared baking pan and sprinkle with marjoram, chili powder, salt, and ground black pepper.
5. Combine the remaining ingredients in a large bowl. Stir to mix well. Pour the mixture over the pork in the pan.
6. Arrange the pan in the preheated oven and bake for 15 minutes or until frothy and the cheese melts. Stir the mixture halfway through.
7. Serve immediately.

Asparagus Frittata with Goat Cheese

Prep time: 5 minutes | Cook time: 25 minutes | Serves 2 to 4

1 cup asparagus spears, cut into 1-inch pieces
1 teaspoon vegetable oil
1 tablespoon milk

6 eggs, beaten
2 ounces (57 g) goat cheese, crumbled
1 tablespoon minced chives, optional
Kosher salt and pepper, to taste

1. Preheat the oven to 400ºF (204ºC).
2. Add the asparagus spears to a small bowl and drizzle with the vegetable oil. Toss until well coated and transfer to a cake pan.
3. Place the pan in the oven. Bake for 5 minutes, or until the asparagus become tender and slightly wilted. Remove then pan from the oven.
4. Stir together the milk and eggs in a medium bowl. Pour the mixture over the asparagus in the pan. Sprinkle with the goat cheese and the chives (if using) over the eggs. Season with a pinch of salt and pepper.
5. Place the pan back to the oven and bake at 320ºF (160ºC) for 20 minutes or until the top is lightly golden and the eggs are set.
6. Transfer to a serving dish. Slice and serve.

Spinach and Mushroom Frittata

Prep time: 7 minutes | Cook time: 8 minutes | Serves 2

1 cup chopped mushrooms
2 cups spinach, chopped
4 eggs, lightly beaten
3 ounces (85 g) feta cheese, crumbled

2 tablespoons heavy cream
A handful of fresh parsley, chopped
Salt and ground black pepper, to taste
Cooking spray

1. Preheat the oven to 350ºF (177ºC). Spritz a baking pan with cooking spray.
2. Whisk together all the ingredients in a large bowl. Stir to mix well.
3. Pour the mixture in the prepared baking pan and place the pan in the preheated oven.
4. Bake for 8 minutes or until the eggs are set.
5. Serve immediately.

Shrimp and Cauliflower Casserole

Prep time: 15 minutes | Cook time: 22 minutes | Serves 4

1 pound (454 g) shrimp, cleaned and deveined
2 cups cauliflower, cut into florets
2 green bell pepper, sliced

1 shallot, sliced
2 tablespoons sesame oil
1 cup tomato paste
Cooking spray

1. Preheat the oven to 360ºF (182ºC). Spritz a baking pan with cooking spray.
2. Arrange the shrimp and vegetables in the baking pan. Then, drizzle the sesame oil over the vegetables. Pour the tomato paste over the vegetables.
3. Bake for 10 minutes in the preheated oven. Stir with a large spoon and bake for a further 12 minutes.
4. Serve warm.

Parmesan Green Bean Casserole

Prep time: 4 minutes | Cook time: 6 minutes | Serves 4

1 tablespoon melted butter
1 cup green beans
6 ounces (170 g) Cheddar cheese, shredded

7 ounces (198 g) Parmesan cheese, shredded
¼ cup heavy cream
Sea salt, to taste

1. Preheat the oven to 400ºF (204ºC). grease a baking pan with the melted butter.
2. Add the green beans, Cheddar, salt, and black pepper to the prepared baking pan. Stir to mix well, then spread the Parmesan and cream on top.
3. Place the baking pan in the preheated oven. Bake for 6 minutes or until the beans are tender and the cheese melts.
4. Serve immediately.

Parmesan Shrimp Quiche

Prep time: 15 minutes | Cook time: 20 minutes | Serves 2

2 teaspoons vegetable oil
4 large eggs
½ cup half-and-half
4 ounces (113 g) raw shrimp, chopped
1 cup shredded Parmesan or Swiss cheese

¼ cup chopped scallions
1 teaspoon sweet smoked paprika
1 teaspoon herbes de Provence
1 teaspoon black pepper
½ to 1 teaspoon kosher salt

1. Preheat the oven to 300ºF (149ºC). Generously grease a round baking pan with 4-inch sides with vegetable oil.
2. In a large bowl, beat together the eggs and half-and-half. Add the shrimp, ¾ cup of the cheese, the scallions, paprika, herbes de Provence, pepper, and salt. Stir with a fork to thoroughly combine. Pour the egg mixture into the prepared pan.
3. Put the pan in the oven and bake for 20 minutes. After 17 minutes, sprinkle the remaining ¼ cup cheese on top and bake for the remaining 3 minutes, or until the cheese has melted, the eggs are set, and a toothpick inserted into the center comes out clean.
4. Serve the quiche warm.

Swiss Chicken and Ham Casserole

Prep time: 15 minutes | Cook time: 15 minutes | Serves 4 to 6

2 cups diced cooked chicken
1 cup diced ham
¼ teaspoon ground nutmeg
½ cup half-and-half

½ teaspoon ground black pepper
6 slices Swiss cheese
Cooking spray

1. Preheat the oven to 350ºF (177ºC). Spritz a baking pan with cooking spray.
2. Combine the chicken, ham, nutmeg, half-and-half, and ground black pepper in a large bowl. Stir to mix well.
3. Pour half of the mixture into the baking pan, then top the mixture with 3 slices of Swiss cheese, then pour in the remaining mixture and top with remaining cheese slices.
4. Arrange the baking pan in the preheated oven and bake for 15 minutes or until the egg is set and the cheese melts.
5. Serve immediately.

Appendix 1: Measurement Conversion Chart

VOLUME EQUIVALENTS(DRY)

US STANDARD	METRIC (APPROXIMATE)
1/8 teaspoon	0.5 mL
1/4 teaspoon	1 mL
1/2 teaspoon	2 mL
3/4 teaspoon	4 mL
1 teaspoon	5 mL
1 tablespoon	15 mL
1/4 cup	59 mL
1/2 cup	118 mL
3/4 cup	177 mL
1 cup	235 mL
2 cups	475 mL
3 cups	700 mL
4 cups	1 L

VOLUME EQUIVALENTS(LIQUID)

US STANDARD	US STANDARD (OUNCES)	METRIC (APPROXIMATE)
2 tablespoons	1 fl.oz.	30 mL
1/4 cup	2 fl.oz.	60 mL
1/2 cup	4 fl.oz.	120 mL
1 cup	8 fl.oz.	240 mL
1 1/2 cup	12 fl.oz.	355 mL
2 cups or 1 pint	16 fl.oz.	475 mL
4 cups or 1 quart	32 fl.oz.	1 L
1 gallon	128 fl.oz.	4 L

TEMPERATURES EQUIVALENTS

FAHRENHEIT(F)	CELSIUS(C) (APPROXIMATE)
225 °F	107 °C
250 °F	120 °C
275 °F	135 °C
300 °F	150 °C
325 °F	160 °C
350 °F	180 °C
375 °F	190 °C
400 °F	205 °C
425 °F	220 °C
450 °F	235 °C
475 °F	245 °C
500 °F	260 °C

WEIGHT EQUIVALENTS

US STANDARD	METRIC (APPROXIMATE)
1 ounce	28 g
2 ounces	57 g
5 ounces	142 g
10 ounces	284 g
15 ounces	425 g
16 ounces (1 pound)	455 g
1.5 pounds	680 g
2 pounds	907 g

Appendix 2: Recipe Index